Mountain and Plain

Mountain and Plain

From the Lycian Coast to the Phrygian Plateau in the Late Roman and Early Byzantine Period

by Martin Harrison

edited by Wendy Young

Ann Arbor

THE UNIVERSITY OF MICHIGAN PRESS

Copyright © by the University of Michigan 2001
All rights reserved
Published in the United States of America by
The University of Michigan Press
⊗ Printed on acid-free paper

2003   2002   2001   2000   4   3   2   1

A CIP catalog record for this book is available from the British Library.

Library of Congress Cataloging-in-Publication Data

Harrison, R. M. (R. Martin), 1935–
    Mountain and plain : from the Lycian coast to the Phrygian plateau in the late Roman
and early Byzantine period / by Martin Harrison ; edited by Wendy Young.
        p.   cm.
    Posthumous work based on the author's notes which were sorted and edited by Wendy Young.
    Includes bibliographical references and index.
    ISBN 0-472-11084-5 (cloth : alk. paper)
    1. Lycia — Antiquities, Roman.   2. Romans — Turkey — Lycia.   3. Lycia — Antiquities,
Byzantine.   4. Greeks — Turkey — Lycia — History — To 1500.   5. Excavations (Archaeology) —
Turkey — Lycia.   6. Phrygia — Antiquities, Roman.   7. Romans — Turkey — Phrygia.
8. Phrygia — Antiquities, Byzantine.   9. Greeks — Turkey — Phrygia — History — To 1500.
10. Excavations (Archaeology) — Turkey — Phrygia.   I. Young, Wendy (Wendy Dennis).
II. Title.

DS156.L8 H37   2001
939′.28 — dc21   00-068266

Foreword

Stephen Hill

At the time of his death on 9 September 1992 Martin Harrison was fifty-seven and in the midst of archaeological affairs. He had returned to England only two weeks previously from directing the sixth season of excavations at Amorium and was full of plans for the future. He was working on a book which sought to connect the themes which he had pursued in his archaeological fieldwork and research in Turkey, and this volume seeks to present some of his ideas — ideas which others have been following through and hopefully will continue to pursue.

This is an unusual volume. It is based extremely closely on notes left by Martin Harrison, and these have been sorted and edited into shape by Wendy Young, who has provided footnotes and references throughout whilst striving to retain the text as closely as possible to that which Martin wrote. Time has passed since these notes were composed, but the volume serves to present to a wider audience some of the ideas with which Martin was working just before his untimely death. As befits what were preliminary notes rather than a fully crafted academic volume, the style and content of this volume is eclectic. At most times the archaeological scholar and field-worker is dominant, but there are strong undertones of the travel writer and copious signs of Martin's interest in the lives and activities of the many people he met and conversed with during his journeys. Like Martin's work as a whole, the volume is in a real sense unfinished, especially the chapter dealing with Amorium, but even that chapter is valuable for the light it casts on the commencement of that venture and for demonstrating the fundamental questions concerning transitions in Byzantine history for which Martin looked to Amorium to supply the answers.

The rationale for the volume is set out by Martin in chapter 4.

I have thus studied three samples of late Roman and Byzantine material, from Constantinople, Lycia, and Amorium—from the capital, mountain villages, and a city on the plateau. I hope to be able to link them somehow.

The links between Lycia and Amorium are explored in this volume: one of the links between all three areas is that together they form a journey which maps the course of the development of Martin's research. As such this journey deserves some exploration here.

Martin Harrison was born on 16 May 1935 into a family which sought to trace its ancestry back to John Harrison, famous clockmaker and recorder of longitude. Clocks and mapping were to be two of Martin's interests throughout his life. Martin was educated at Sherborne School and then at Lincoln College, Oxford, where he read Greats. In 1954 he went on a trip to Chios intending to sketch and to paint watercolors—the latter being another of his lifelong interests, as is demonstrated by surviving paintings of the mosaics at Alahan and Al Oda. But in Chios he became involved in the excavations being conducted by the British School at Athens. The year 1955 saw him in Turkey; more particularly, he went to the great early Byzantine pilgrimage site of Alahan in the Isaurian Taurus, where he worked on the excavations directed by Michael Gough. This episode secured Martin's lifelong personal and professional interests in and commitment to Turkey and the Turks and his specialization in late Roman and early Byzantine archaeology. After Michael Gough's early death, Martin was to contribute a major chapter, on "the inscriptions and chronology of Alahan," to Mary Gough's publication of her husband's work (*Alahan, an Early Christian Monastery in Southern Turkey* [Toronto, 1985]).

Martin began serious fieldwork in Lycia in 1959. He was accompanied by his new wife, Elizabeth, who was to be a constant encourager and supporter and who worked as photographer through the long seasons of fieldwork in Lycia and the excavations at Saraçhane in Istanbul. Elizabeth's photographs were included in Martin's major publication "Churches and Chapels of Central Lycia," which appeared in *Anatolian Studies* 13 (1963): 117–51. This and a later article, "A Note on Architectural Sculpture in Central Lycia" (*Anatolian Studies* 22 [1972]: 187–97) still stand as noteworthy records of a significant and architecturally important group of early Byzantine churches. Martin's article in 1963 brought to the world's attention major monuments such as the monastic establishments at Karabel, which are here linked with St. Nicholas of Sion (see app. 1).

In his early surveys in upland Lycia, Martin's attention was drawn to the well-preserved domestic structures that form a major focus in chapter 2 of this volume. Though the Lycian material was the least published aspect of his work, the notes he left behind show that Martin was thinking creatively about it in his final years. His first publications on Lycia display Martin's interest in ecclesiastical architecture and architectural sculpture — the traditional fodder of early Byzantinists. Martin was thoroughly competent in these fields and retained his interest in them, as may be seen from the fact that he was still working on the sculpture from Saraçhane at the end of his life; but I well remember how, when I was working on the research for my Ph.D. on the ecclesiastical architecture of Cilicia, Martin exhorted me to move on from churches and their architecture and sculptural decoration to "more important" things such as domestic architecture and settlement patterns. His suggestion was not followed through, for, as Martin was well aware, Byzantinists need their churches as landmarks for dating other structures. In making the suggestion, however, he was prescient of the way archaeology was to expand and develop. Martin moved on, but the rest of us did not move so quickly. The results of this shift in the emphasis of Martin's fieldwork in Lycia may be seen in the discussions of the domestic architecture of Alakilise in chapter 2 of this volume. This aspect of his work was presented in a small number of conference proceedings but was destined not to be brought together fully in print. The material presented here at least fills out some of the record and thus helps us to place Lycia in a broader context, for there has been recent work conducted by Stephen Mitchell, Jim Coulton, and others on the classical and late Roman settlements of adjoining Pisidia, whilst the monuments of equivalent provinces of Cilicia and Isauria, oft referred to in Martin's notes here, have also been the subject of considerable recent study (see the supplementary bibliography).

The early 1960s saw Martin employed in various ways. He was controller of antiquities in Cyrenaica in 1960–61. That his main interest was by then in the early Byzantine period is well evidenced by his work on the churches of Ras-el-Hilal and Cyrene. He next spent a brief period in the United States lecturing at Bryn Mawr, where he formed a lasting friendship with another great Lycian scholar, Machteld Mellink. In 1963 he went back to Lincoln College as Glanville Scholar, and in 1964 he was appointed to a lectureship in Roman archaeology in the Classics Department of the University of Newcastle upon Tyne. Martin was to remain at that post in Newcastle for twenty-one years, succeeding Sir Ian Richmond as professor of Roman archaeology in 1968 and, in 1972, becoming founder professor of the newly established Department of Archaeology. Throughout much of this time, he was ably supported by his research assistant Wendy Young (formerly Dennis), who has edited this volume.

The early years at Newcastle saw Martin's program of excavation at the church of St. Polyeuktos at Saraçhane in Istanbul. The site was discovered as a result of bulldozing for the new Atatürk Bulvarı, which links Aksaray with the Golden Horn via Saraçhane and the Aqueduct of Valens. It was not easy work for the archaeologists, since road building continued and the excavation was conducted underneath the still live main power cable of the city. Moving the massive fallen blocks of the church was a minor engineering triumph in its own right. The program of excavations lasted from 1964 to 1969: it was supported financially by the Dumbarton Oaks Byzantine Research Center, Washington, D.C., and was conducted in happy collaboration with the late Dr. Nezih Fıratlı, director of the Istanbul Museum. These years of collaboration bore all sorts of different fruit: Martin and Nezih conducted a sondage around the feet of one of the piers of the Aqueduct of Valens, and the opportunity was taken to conduct a preliminary survey of the Long Walls of Thrace. The main fruit of this period was the uncovering of the remains of the great church of St. Polyeuktos which was constructed by Anicia Juliana and completed in the early years of Justinian's reign. It was an architectural wonder, doubtless domed, and yet predating the famous Justinianic "domed basilicas" which have been the subject of so much admiration and speculation on the part of architectural historians. There is another thread in the story here, for Alahan and Karabel are also important links in the architectural saga which led to the creation of Justinian's church of Santa Sophia. The design and decoration of St. Polyeuktos mark it out as something very special in early Byzantine architecture, and Martin was particularly interested in chasing the art historical aspects of the Saraçhane sculpture back to Sassanian origins, but it was the scale of the church which was particularly remarkable. Martin detected various sculptural elements at Saraçhane which resembled known elements from the Temple of Solomon and was also able to show that it was one hundred royal cubits square in direct imitation of Solomon's Temple. He was quick to point out that St. Polyeuktos was the biggest church in Constantinople at the time of Justinian's accession, and he delighted in the tales of Anicia Juliana, dowager member of the traditional imperial family, outsmarting the upstart Justinian — small wonder, then, that Justinian was credited with exclaiming, when his great church was completed, "Solomon, I have defeated thee."

For Byzantine archaeologists and art historians the excavations at Saraçhane still hold a position of great honor. The formal final report, *Excavations at Saraçhane in Istanbul,* appeared as two fat volumes in 1986 and 1992. Between them, these volumes record exhaustively the architecture, sculpture, pottery, coins, brickstamps, and other small and large finds which were rescued from the site and which form and will continue to form the type series for so many subsequent studies of Constantinopolitan archaeology. But the "popular" publication of Saraçhane, *A Temple for Byzantium,* which appeared in 1989, is in many ways an equally important study of the church, for it includes Martin's more mature thoughts on the significance of the building and has the additional merit of being lavishly illustrated in color.

As a would-be graduate student in the early 1970s, I asked my tutor in St. Andrews, Professor Geoffrey Rickman, where to go to study Byzantine archaeology. The reply was discouraging — "There isn't really such a subject, but you could try going to Newcastle to study with Martin Harrison." Martin's fame at that time depended on Saraçhane, and to Martin and St. Polyeuktos must be awarded the distinction of establishing Byzantine archaeology as a subject which could be offered to students in Britain. Martin's excavations at Saraçhane were simply the biggest thing that had happened to Byzantine archaeology in Britain, eclipsing even the Russell and Walker Trusts' excavations of the Great Palace of the Byzantine Emperors. I did indeed try going to Newcastle, where I was greeted heartily and enthusiastically by a tall and cheerful man in a black beret. The study of Byzantine archaeology is an honorable British tradition, and Martin will be remembered as one of its giant figures for directing an excavation on a scale that is unlikely to be seen again on a major monument in Constantinople.

After the excavations at Saraçhane were completed, there were long seasons of postexcavation work in the, frankly, unlovely depot which was formed from the substructures of the church of St. Polyeuktos. At the ends of these seasons Martin would sometimes go back to his roots and return to Lycia. I had the privilege, with my wife, Fiona, to accompany him on one of these journeys in 1975. The climb to Alakilise, conducted by the light of a full moon between midnight and the early morning, was unforgettable. Martin still had the beret, but it was accompanied now by a walking stick, which had become necessary following a car crash in Northumberland. Despite a newly acquired limp, he stoutly ascended the *boş merkep yolu* (empty donkey road) with enthusiasm and alacrity, and we spent a second unforgettable night under the stars, on the veranda of the Akkaya family house. That journey, too, involved a visit to Elmalı and from there to Ovacık, where this lesser mortal got sunstroke from carrying the fragments of the inscription (which forms the subject of appendix 2) back to Martin's elderly Dormobile. En route back to Istanbul we paused to visit the site of Amorium, for Martin, much inspired by Cyril Mango, was beginning to cherish the notion that the site of this formerly great city held the key to the mysteries

of the transition from Classical to Byzantine. Martin was later to observe
that this trip in 1975 marked the beginning of his working coherently toward
a book on changing settlement patterns in southern late Roman and Byzantine Asia Minor. This volume is the end product of those thought processes.

Martin returned to work in Lycia during the late 1970s and early 1980s,
working particularly at Alakilise and Arif, with Gordon Lawson, who had
also served as architectural draughtsman at Saraçhane. In 1985 he moved to
the chair of Roman archaeology in the Institute of Archaeology at Oxford,
being elected also to a fellowship at All Souls. Tragically, in his first year at
Oxford, Martin suffered a serious stroke, which, for a time, made it very
difficult for him to communicate verbally, though he bravely returned to
learning to play the cello at this time. Characteristically, he refused to let this
further disability get in the way of his research. The first volume of Saraçhane
reports appeared in 1986, and in 1987 he conducted the first season of excavation at Amorium. This project was to occupy him for the rest of his life, and
the questions which he was anxious to answer are set out lucidly in chapter 4.

Questions are, in a real sense, what this volume is about. The reader will
find questions about why Lycian cities declined after the fifth century, about
the relationship between coastal cities and upland villages, about the economy of monastic communities in late antiquity, about Holy Mountains and
their influence, about patronage and architectural development, and finally
about settlement continuity which Martin sought in the Anatolian plateau,
having failed to find it in Lycia. The questions which Martin posed are not all
answered, though further studies in Lycia and in other parts of southern Asia
Minor have confirmed the patterns which he defined for Lycia, whilst continued excavation at Amorium has confirmed the importance of that site into the
ninth and tenth centuries, exactly as Martin expected.

Stephen Hill, December 1998

Editor's Note and Acknowledgments

A paragraph in George Eliot's *Middlemarch* describes the heroine, Dorothea, as follows: "Was there not the geography of Asia Minor, in which her slackness had often been rebuked. . . . She went to the cabinet of maps . . . and fixed her total darkness . . . on the shores of Euxine." This account could have equally applied to myself when I began to work with Martin Harrison in 1972. My contribution toward his Lycian research initially involved preparing reports, but after he suffered a stroke in 1985, I became his research assistant to enable him to produce a book on the subject. The book was virtually complete when, sadly, Martin died in 1992. With constant support and encouragement from his wife, Elizabeth, I have made slight amendments to the text and provided notes and bibliography.

My grateful thanks are due to Elizabeth Harrison for her assistance in all respects and particularly with illustrations; to Michael Ballance and Charlotte Roueché for appendix 2, "Three Inscriptions from Ovacık"; to Stephen Hill for the foreword; to Allan Jones and Pat Knox for assistance with maps; to Machteld Mellink for considerable help with the Elmalı plateau; and to the Amorium excavation team, to Patrick Browne, Mark Hide, Gordon Lawson, Cyril Mango, Stephen Mitchell, James Morganstern, Lynn Ritchie, Pat Southern, Tolga Tek, and, last but certainly not least, my husband, Tom. In addition, the library of the Ashmolean Museum, Oxford, kindly allowed me access and thus considerably eased my search for references.

Grateful acknowledgment is made to Jean Greenhalgh for permission to quote from her doctoral thesis, to the Hellenic College Press for permission to include extracts from the *Life of St. Nicholas of Sion* by I. Ševčenko and N. P. Ševčenko, and to Cyril Mango for his translation of the inscription on the sarcophagus lid from Islâmlar. Unless otherwise stated, the drawings, plans, and photographs are Martin Harrison's. Others were kindly contributed by Vicki Frenz, Margaret Gill, Gordon Lawson, and James Morganstern.

Wendy Young

Author's Preface and Introduction

This book will describe an archaeological study of change and development in Lycia and Phrygia (ancient provinces of what is now modern Turkey), beginning on the south coast and moving northward and inland via the Lycian mountains to the central plateau of Anatolia. The survey will commence in late Roman and early Byzantine times and continue down through the Byzantine period, including the so-called Dark Ages. The study of these Dark Ages (ca. A.D. 610–850) is popular at present, in Britain, Italy, and elsewhere. Asia Minor (or Turkey) may be particularly important in throwing some new light on the subject. The eminent Byzantinist Sir Steven Runciman has written:

> Byzantine studies are on the way to becoming the belle of the academic ball. Let us hope that Classical Greek and Classical Roman studies, who have dominated the dance-floor for so long, will not find themselves in the role of the Ugly Sisters, outshone by the Cinderella of Byzantium.[1]

In the Roman period, there were about 350 towns in the province of Asia Minor, most of which were in the west and south. Some of these were Roman foundations, and many were Hellenistic, but the majority were probably earlier. During the Roman period and the Dark Ages, the larger and smaller towns, both on the coast and inland, were subject to change and development at different periods and for a variety of reasons. In Asia Minor a particular problem was the silting up of harbors, resulting from the deposition of riverborne alluvium. Another problem was the outbreak of bubonic plague, which occurred about every fifteen years, with a particularly serious outbreak in A.D. 542. A third problem resulted from the reduction in efficiency of the civic authorities, which was accompanied by increasing taxes. There was an associated loss of function of amenities, such as aqueducts, baths, sewers, and bread supplies. This decline occurred simultaneously

---

1. Runciman 1986, 5.

with the development of the city of Constantinople, which reached a peak in about A.D. 500, and which may have been a contributory factor; it has been estimated that at that time, Constantinople covered some fourteen hundred hectares and had a population of three hundred thousand to four hundred thousand people.[2] In addition, during the seventh century, many cities were destroyed, first by the Persians and then by the Arabs, through regular attacks both by land and sea.[3]

This study has been organized to start with the coastal cities, including Myra; move inland to the Lycian mountains; then look at the high plateau around Elmalı; and finally travel a much greater distance, to Amorium in Phrygia. I will thus cover a cross section of the country from the south to the center, illustrating the ways in which different areas adapted to changing situations.

I traveled in central Lycia with my wife in 1959, 1960, and 1963. In 1977, 1979, 1980, and 1982, I worked there with Gordon Lawson (architect) and various Turkish representatives, whose helpful assistance is remembered with gratitude. In 1982, Ann Thorley (botanist), Derrick Webley (geomorphologist), and Hazel Dodge (archaeologist) also assisted me. My wife and members of my family went to Lycia with me in 1984, 1985, and 1986.

Funds for my research in Lycia were provided by the British Institute of Archaeology at Ankara (1959–60), Dumbarton Oaks (1977, 1979, and 1980), and the British Academy (1963 and 1982). I am most grateful to Cevdet Bayburtluoğlu, Machteld Mellink, and Henri Metzger; to many other colleagues; and to the villagers, particularly to the Akkaya family at Alakilise. My work at Amorium is funded by the British Academy, the University of Oxford, and a number of other societies and trusts.

Martin Harrison, March 1990

2: Mango 1980, 75.
3. Foss 1975, 721–47; 1976.

Contents

Abbreviations

ACLA	*Actes du Colloque sur la Lycie Antique.* Bibliothèque de l'Institut Français d'Etudes Anatoliennes d'Istanbul, vol. 27. Paris, 1980.
AJA	*American Journal of Archaeology*
Arch. Anz.	*Archäologischer Anzeiger*
AS	*Anatolian Studies*
CRAI	*Comptes Rendus des Séances de l'Année 1979 avril-juin.* Académie des Inscriptions et Belles-Lettres, Paris, 1979.
JRS	*Journal of Roman Studies*
MAMA	*Monumenta Asiae Minoris Antiqua*
PBSR	*Papers of the British School at Rome*
RA	*Revue Archéologique*

Guide to Chronological Periods

Hittite Empire	ca. 1400–1200 B.C.
Classical	ca. 479–323 B.C.
Hellenistic	ca. 323–130 B.C.
Roman	ca. 129 B.C.–A.D. 330
Late Roman/ late antique/ early Byzantine	ca. late third to early/mid–seventh century A.D. (these terms are used pretty much indiscriminately)
Dark Ages	A.D. 610–850
Middle Byzantine	ca. A.D. 850–1204 (for Asia Minor it may be more realistic to restrict this to 1071, prior to the Selcuk invasion)
Selcuk	A.D. 1071 until late thirteenth century
Late Byzantine	ca. A.D. 1204–1453
Ottoman/Turkish	ca. A.D. 1453–1923
Modern Turkish	A.D. 1923 until present day

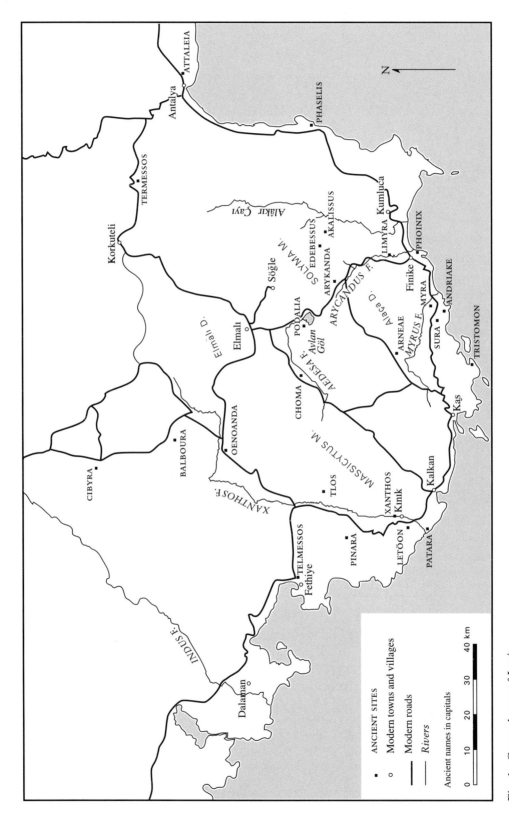

Fig. 1. General map of Lycia

Chapter 1

Cities of the Lycian Coastal Region

The province of Lycia occupied a broad, rugged promontory some 130 kilometers across, extending from the Indus River (Dalaman Çayı) in the west toward Attaleia (Antalya) in the east. To the west was the province of Caria, to the east was that of Pamphylia, and to the north and east was Pisidia. The Lycian mountains rise steeply from the sea to summits exceeding three thousand meters in height. They form two principal massifs, Akdağ (the ancient Massicytus) in the west and Bey Dağ (the ancient Solyma) in the east. The central plateau of Elmalı is about eleven hundred meters above sea level. Six main rivers flow through the mountains to the coast, which in the main is steep and rocky. But at four points—Phoinix (Finike), Myra (Demre), the valley of the river Xanthos (Eşen Çayı), and Telmessos (Fethiye)—the terrain levels out into small coastal plains. These plains are largely of recent formation, the sea having receded since classical times, and in each place deep alluvial silt probably conceals a deepwater harbor. The shoreline is extremely rugged, and thirty years ago there was no coastal road. Strabo commented that Lycia was "difficult and dangerous but [had] good harbors,"[1] and, indeed, it is recorded that St. Paul changed ships at Myra on his journey from Syria to Rome.[2] George Bean suggested that the population of Lycia in the second century A.D. was perhaps two hundred thousand.[3] It is probably about the same now, if one excludes the growing hordes of tourists that swarm along the coasts in summer.

In classical times, the Lycian province supported as many as forty cities. Some of these, which were situated on or near the coast, were of considerable size and importance. Perhaps they owed their prosperity to the fact that the main shipping lanes from Syria and Egypt to the west followed their shore, with its good harbors. However, in late antiquity, probably after the

---

1. Strabo *Geography* 14.3.
2. Acts of the Apostles 27:5–6.
3. Bean 1978, 19.

fifth century, these cities are thought to have declined, while many new smaller settlements (monasteries, villages, or even towns) appeared in the mountain valleys further inland. One of the most interesting questions about this area is whether this development is characteristic of the whole southern coast or simply due to the existence of a holy mountain, now known as Alaca Dağ? The coast had not been abandoned; indeed, there was a kind of mutual dependence between it and the inland settlements. However, in this later period, the population of the coastal cities was probably smaller. Their churches were built of reused stone, and civic amenities, such as piped water and even food supplies, were probably scarcer. By contrast, in the hills were villages and monasteries with excellent stonework, sculpture, and, in the case of the Sion monastery, silver treasure and gold coins. The population of Alaca Dağ numbered thousands rather than hundreds. The ancient upland landscape is well preserved and has been little exploited archaeologically. It is an ideal subject for an examination of the questions of continuity and change at this critical period.

The first archaeological map of Lycia was drawn in 1842 by Spratt and Forbes,[4] who traveled around the area on horseback for three months. Using scientific tables, they calculated the heights of the elevated plains by observing the temperature of the boiling point of water, taking always the mean of the readings shown on two thermometers. In addition, their alidade was fairly accurate, and their calculations are said to be only between fifteen and thirty meters in error, where they were estimating heights of over three thousand meters. Their map is extraordinarily correct. For comparison, a satellite photograph of the area taken in the 1980s shows remarkably few differences. Their book gives rich details of archaeological remains, including inscriptions, together with faunal, botanical, and other observations. The cities described by Spratt and Forbes have only very recently become the subject of archaeological research.

Pinara

Pinara was one of the leading cities of the coastal area. Its acropolis, lower city, Roman agora, and theater were well surveyed in the 1970s by Wurster, who also did similar surveys on Tlos, Apollonia, Candyba, Limyra, and other cities.[5] He drew plans of the Archaic, Roman, Byzantine (or, more accurately, late Roman/early Byzantine) periods of the city, but there seems to be

---

4. Spratt and Forbes 1847, 1:xviii.
5. Wurster 1976, 23–49; Wurster and Wörrle 1978, 74–101.

little archaeological evidence arising from the Dark Ages and later Byzantine periods. However, his report is clear and useful. The city flourished and expanded during the Roman period and then contracted as the population fell.

Xanthos

A similar pattern seems to emerge from a study of Xanthos, on the river of the same name. Its site is now ten kilometers away from the sea, due to the deposition of riverborne alluvium. The city has been studied by a French excavation team, who have worked on the site since the 1950s.[6] The original city was centered on a high acropolis, and a succession of building periods followed on that site. The Hellenistic and Roman city spread east and north to incorporate a higher hill and a vast area; in late antiquity it shrank to a small, strongly fortified nucleus on the original acropolis.

The fortification of the north side of the acropolis in the early Byzantine period consisted of a solid wall incorporating three major triangular towers,[7] of a type also seen at Thessalonika,[8] Serdica,[9] and Amorium,[10] where the tower was dated to the late Roman period (see chap. 4). It would be interesting to know whether these three towers were sixth or seventh century in date or even later.

In the area of the Roman agora and theater are some important earlier Lycian tombs. The so-called Harpy Tomb has a large base, surmounted by a pillar, which supports a marble grave chamber decorated with reliefs, some of which illustrate strange bird-women; the whole structure stands twenty-five feet high. The Obelisk is in fact a straightforward pillar tomb, which carries an inscription of over 250 lines in two variants of the Lycian language and a short passage in Greek.

The classical city at Xanthos was built of well-cut limestone and decorated with fine sculpture of the fifth and fourth centuries B.C. For example, the Nereid Tomb, dating to the fifth century B.C., had rich sculpture, most of which was taken to the British Museum in the nineteenth century. Later, there were fine Hellenistic and Roman buildings, including the Gate of Vespasian in the lower city. Construction was mainly in good local ashlar, which can be seen in cornices and other sculpture.

6. Demargne et al., 1958–; Demargne and Metzger 1966.
7. Metzger 1963, 1–2, pl. 7.
8. Spieser 1984, 74–76.
9. Bobčev 1961, 103–45.
10. Harrison 1989a, 171; 1990, 211–13, pl. XXXIIIb; 1991, 220–22, fig. 4, pl. XLIIIb; Harrison et al. 1993, 150–51, pl. XXVIIA.

In comparison, a small Christian basilica erected in the late Roman period as part of the reorganization of the agora incorporated reused masonry in its construction. In addition, the large church in the eastern quarter of Xanthos excavated by Jean-Pierre Sodini[11] had an apse built of reused blocks taken from the earlier necropolis, and the main walls were not of ashlar but of rough stone and mortar. The jambs and lintels of the three north doorways were recarved from building material of the second or early third century A.D.

This large Christian basilica was constructed in about the fifth century. On its northeast side was a small *triconchos* (or clover-leaf-shaped) chapel with distinctive sculpture, now broken into many pieces, of about eleventh-century date. However, there appears to be no evidence of continuity during the five hundred years between these two dates.

The Letöon, about six kilometers to the south of Xanthos, was a religious sanctuary dedicated to Leto, the mother of Apollo and Artemis. Its temples, stoas, theater, and *nymphaeum* are mainly of Hellenistic and Roman date, but there is also a church (possibly a monastery) with a classical column drum reused as the altar.[12] Other reused materials, including classical inscriptions, were built into its stonework. There are good pavements of mosaic and *opus sectile,* but decorative sculpture is crude in the extreme. At the time of the construction of this church, the three Hellenistic temples in the sanctuary had already been destroyed and the Roman semicircular basin nearby had gone out of use. The evidence of coins and pottery indicates that the church was built in about the early sixth century A.D., and it seems to have lasted for about a hundred years or slightly longer.

Myra

Myra was another coastal city that enjoyed major importance in the Roman period.[13] Almost the whole area of the city is now covered by between five and eight meters of alluvial silt, and the modern shoreline is some five kilometers away.

The principal building now visible at Myra is the theater,[14] near the acropolis. It is second century in date, very large, and well built, and its *scaenae frons* (the wall of the stage building) includes marble columns imported from outside Lycia. There were about five meters of alluvium

---

11. Metzger 1971, 58; Sodini 1970–74. For a plan, see *ACLA* (1980): 120.
12. Harrison 1996, 109–11.
13. Borchhardt 1975b.
14. Ibid., 57–60, pls. 18–27.

inside the theater until it was dug out in the 1960s. The face of the alluvial deposit remaining in the arches of the stage building, shows fifty or more thin layers of red and gray earth, each less than a centimeter thick, laid down after the theater had gone out of use. The alluvium was thus deposited not suddenly in one year but over some time. It was probably deposited each autumn and spring over fifty or one hundred years or more. The red and gray colors could represent red limestone alluvium from the mountain of Alaca Dağ (including the areas of Muskar, Alakilise, and Karabel) and gray silty soil from the slopes around Dereağzı and Arneae, washed down in autumn rains and by melting snow in the spring. An impressive collection of rock-cut tombs of various types and sizes occupies the steep cliff above the theater.

The second important building visible today is the Granary of Hadrian,[15] outside the walls of Myra, at the port of Andriake. It is excellently built of large limestone ashlar, and the whole structure is preserved except for its wooden roof. It is sixty-one meters long and has inscriptions and sculpture. The building was still in use in the late fourth century, when an inscription was cut in its wall to record that the praetorian prefect had been sent standards of weights and measures for use in Myra and Arneae (another city nearby).

A third building, now cleared of alluvium, is the church of St. Nicholas,[16] founded originally in the sixth century A.D. or earlier, which probably lay outside the city walls. The present building possibly dates from the ninth century, and restorations were carried out in the eleventh and twelfth centuries, but at some time after that, deposits of waterborne alluvium between six and eight meters in depth accumulated inside and over the church. It was eventually buried by the alluvium and became an underground church and atrium. In the nineteenth century, the main vaults were reconstructed and a small Greek Orthodox chapel was added to the southwest corner. The interior contained good limestone capitals and other sculptures, either placed there in the sixth century or moved there at a later period (figs. 2–4). Such sculptures seem to be exceptional on this coast, and their presence here may be due to the connection with St. Nicholas.

The church was a foot deep under water when Hans Rott did a survey in 1902.[17] I saw it in 1959, before the major part of the building was dug out and put in order in the 1960s, and Professor Yıldız Ötuken has worked there in more recent years.

---

15. Wörrle 1975, 66–71, pls. 35–41.
16. Peschlow 1975, 303–59, pls. 101–30.
17. Rott 1908, 327–41.

Fig. 2. Myra (Demre); church of St. Nicholas, decorative detail

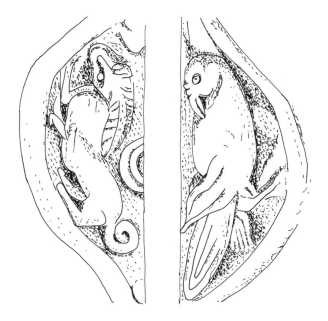

Fig. 3. Myra (Demre); church of St. Nicholas, decorative detail

The church is famous for its association with St. Nicholas, who was bishop of Myra in the early fourth century A.D. After a slow start, his cult spread with extraordinary rapidity in the Middle Ages. Indeed, by the ninth century his legend had become fused with that of the sixth-century abbot Nicholas of Sion, in the territory of Myra (see app. 1).

The city of Myra became increasingly important in the ninth century (after the Arab siege in 809) and again in the eleventh century, as a place of pilgrimage.[18] Then a long decline set in so that no more than a sleepy

18. Harrison 1963, 121–22.

Fig. 4. Myra (Demre); church of St. Nicholas, decorative detail

mosquito-infested village (called Demre) occupied the plain on the seaward side of ancient Myra. However, since the construction of the coastal road in the 1960s, Demre has developed into a small town with taxis, banks, a mosque, cinemas, and asphalt streets.

In the Hellenistic and Roman periods, all three cities exhibit the same pattern of excellent building techniques and good quality masonry and sculpture. However, there is evidence of decline, if not collapse, of the infrastructure in late Roman/early Byzantine times.

The great Hellenistic and Roman cities of the coast give no evidence of new building or any major development much after the fourth century A.D. The inference is that the coastal centers were in decline. However, chapter 2 will show that the mountain valleys in Lycia were clearly enjoying a modest prosperity, with a considerable population despite the terrain, and with a fervor of church and monastery building. Why these settlement changes took place can only be speculated on, but certainly climatic and geographical changes (seen in the silting up of harbors), the economy (including the factors of piracy, taxes, and trade), and disease must have contributed a part. The history of the inland villages and churches of another province of Asia Minor (Isauria) seems relevant, but neither case as yet sheds full light on the Dark Ages.

Chapter 2

From the Coast to the Mountains

Many important religious settlements lay in the mountains above Demre (Myra), including major churches at the modern villages/hamlets of Muskar, Alakilise, Turant, Karabel, Dikmen, and Devekuyusu.[1] There are two routes leading inland from Demre to the mountain site of Arneae. One follows an easy gradient through the gorge to the modern Dereağzı and then winds through rocky cliffs for some fifteen kilometers. The other climbs more directly through the mountains, passing the hamlets of Muskar and Karabel.

Dereağzı

The gorge route was eventually defended by a large Byzantine fortress at Dereağzı, at the point where it reached the Kasaba plateau. A kilometer away is the Dereağzı church, which was discovered by Texier in 1836; visited by several other nineteenth-century travelers, including Benndorf and Niemann; and surveyed by Rott in 1906.[2] I visited the site in 1959, and a full study of the church was made by James Morganstern and published in 1983.[3] It is still an impressive ruin, with the north walls standing to two storys in height (figs. 38–39).

The church has been dated to the late ninth or early tenth century. It is a cross-domed basilica, 38.38 meters long in total and 45.19 meters wide. The main building was entered via an outer narthex and a narthex, and it consists

---

1. I worked in central Lycia in 1959, 1960, and 1963 with my wife. On the first occasion, we traveled for over six months in the province. A donkey carried our large tent and paraphernalia, including books and food. We were given a hundred packets of dried soup and eleven small Christmas puddings before we set out; otherwise we lived on *yufka* (a type of local bread) and tomatoes. We were also given fruit — in June, apricots; in August, melons and grapes. At one place, seven cans of sardines were the only food available for purchase.

2. Texier 1849, 202, 232, pl. CCV; Benndorf and Niemann 1884, 131, pl. XXXVIII; Rott 1908, 300–314.

3. Harrison 1963, 138, pl. XLIV; Morganstern 1983.

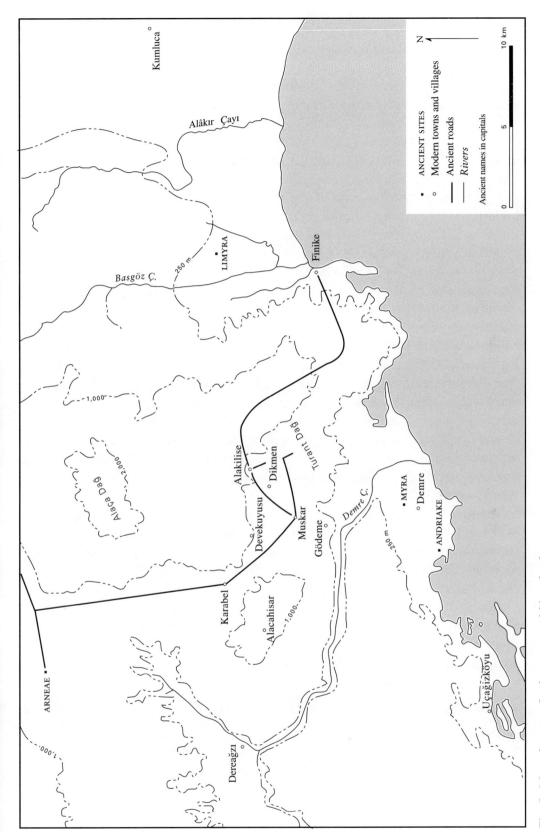

Fig. 5. Map of eastern Lycian coast and hinterland

of a nave divided into three bays, a deep chancel surrounded by elaborate rooms and chapels, and a large segmental apse. A complicated system of walls defined the central area, and an equally complex arrangement of barrel vaults roofed the church, with a dome about eight meters in diameter over the central bay of the nave. A U-shaped gallery over the narthex and side aisles was reached by stairways inside two external turrets. Two octagonal buildings, each about 6.16 meters in diameter internally, stand asymmetrically alongside the church, one to the north, the other to the south. They are single-story constructions with thick walls, and tunnels link them to the main building. Their purpose is not clear, but they seem to have been designed for different functions: the north octagon was a plain, closed-in building containing storage shelves and was possibly a funerary chapel; the south octagon was more elaborate and open, with large windows, and may have been a chapel or baptistery.

Building materials included stone, concrete, and bricks, which were imported from the coasts of the Sea of Marmara or the Dardanelles. Granite columns from the same area and sculpture of Proconnesian marble may have been *spolia*. Other reused architectural fragments included an architrave or cornice resembling fifth/sixth-century sculpture from Alakilise (figs. 11–16) and Muskar (figs. 41–43, 96) and a capital in the Antalya Museum (fig. 44), and other pieces recall sculpture from the church of St. Nicholas at Myra (figs. 2–4). It seems possible that these came from an earlier Christian building on or near the site of the present church, or they may have been brought from elsewhere. The church was also decorated with elaborate painted plaster and mosaics.

The plan of the Dereağzı church is related to several of the most important buildings in Constantinople, including the church of St. Eirene (restored in the mid–eighth century). This impressive building in a remote mountain area may have been related to a reorganization of Lycian bishoprics in the late ninth century, as the seat of a new bishop. Or it may have been a pilgrimage church or part of a monastery. The remains of other buildings surrounding the church may have been the bishop's palace, accommodation for pilgrims, or monastic cells. It is clear, however, that the Dereağzı complex was of major importance.

Muskar

The mountain route from Myra (Demre) followed an ancient track to the hamlets that are now called Gödeme and Muskar. This track was rock-cut and revetted with a rock staircase just above Gödeme (proof, if proof were

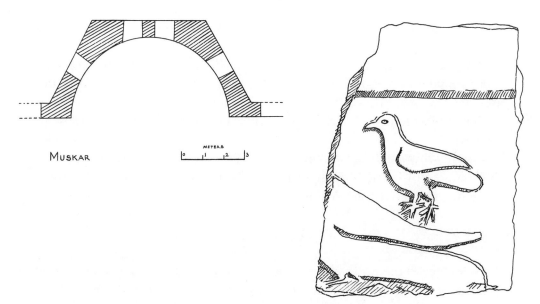

MUSKAR

METERS

Fig. 6. Muskar; plan of apse of church (118° magnetic) and bird
sculpture from neighboring house (upper width = 0.18 m; lower width
= 0.26 m; total height = 0.29 m; thickness = 0.14 m)

needed, that it was not intended for wheeled traffic). The village of Muskar
probably existed in antiquity. It was the meeting place of at least six ancient
roads—those to modern Turant, Alakilise, Devekuyusu, Karabel, Muskar
Castle, and Demre. It is interesting that it is simpler to move horizontally,
traversing the mountains, than it is to move vertically from the mountains to
the coast, because of the very steep gorges and sheer rock faces that are
interposed.[4]

Muskar has a church of about sixth-century date,[5] of which the east end
is virtually intact (figs. 6, 95). It is well constructed in smallish ashlar
blocks. The walls of the apse, which is externally polygonal, rise vertically
to the crown of a semidome, about eight meters above present ground
level. This apse was carefully built and had four horseshoe-shaped arched
windows. Internally, the church had a limestone cornice with enriched acanthus scrolls; the cornice within the apse was punctuated by five equidistant
Maltese crosses (figs. 40–41). An extraordinarily large capital (0.81 m high)
was decorated with vine leaves, bunches of grapes and windblown acanthus. Two smaller capitals also had acanthus sculpture. The presence of

4. Harrison 1979a, 528, pls. 3–4.
5. Rott 1908, 315–16; Harrison 1963, 131, 146, pl. XXXVIe; Harrison 1972, 192–95; Severin 1977,
24; Harrison 1980, 110, pl. XIXb.

these capitals seems to indicate that the nave was divided from the aisles by colonnades (figs. 43, 96; cf. capital in Antalya Museum, fig. 44).

Beyond Muskar, on a ridge above Myra, lie a few Roman sarcophagi. Some remains of massive masonry, including Doric column drums, are situated slightly lower down the slope, to the southeast. Nearby is an ancient settlement including a church, a rectangular building, and the traces of some houses.

Also nearby on a hill is a small castle. It looks toward Myra and the sea to the south and toward Muskar to the north. It was probably a watchtower and a defense against the Arabs.[6]

Alakilise

Alakilise lies to the northeast of Muskar. It is an hour and a half away from Muskar on foot, along a rock-cut and revetted road of both ancient and more recent construction (fig. 45). The ancient village covers the lower slopes of a wide secluded valley that narrows into a gorge leading down to Myra (figs. 7, 46). It was deserted in the winter of 1906, when Rott found a great deal of snow there.[7] However, there are now three modern stone houses in the valley, one of which was built in 1935, while the others are more recent.[8]

The surrounding woodland consists of pine, oak, sandal (or Greek strawberry tree), *pistacea,* storax, myrtle, and, on the higher slopes, cedar of Lebanon.[9] The valley is dry for most of the year, but for a few months in winter there is a rushing torrent along its floor. There are ancient and modern

6. Harrison 1984, 76, figs. 2–5.
7. Rott 1908, 317–24.
8. When I first visited the area, the population consisted of one family, made up of Osman Akkaya, his wife, and their six sons. There is no water in the valley in summer, and they relied on the one intact medieval cistern, which the rains replenished each winter. They sowed the broad valley floor with wheat and reared goats and other livestock in summer, and they spent the winter months at Demre on the coast. In the summer months, some members of the family carried snow wrapped in goat-hair sacks from the northern slopes of Alaca Dağ to Demre, using a camel and donkeys. This snow was used for cooling lemonade. The journey, which was accomplished twice a week, took one day to go down and two days to come back, but when there was a moon it was possible to travel by night. The trade ended in 1960, when the new coast road opened, thus permitting a daily supply of ice to be brought to Demre from Finike. In 1975 only the Akkaya parents and one son and his wife remained, the others having yielded to the attractions of successful orange and tomato growing on the outskirts of Demre. Osman Akkaya, a determined old man with a twinkle in his eye, declared that he would never settle permanently in Demre. He lived in a ramshackle old stone house built against the hillside near the church and his wife and daughter-in-law used the broad veranda to grind flour and bake *yufka,* while he and his son Süleyman looked after the goats, collected wood, and cleared the fields for their sparse harvest. By 1981 all the family had abandoned the area. One of the reasons for their departure was the diminishing water supply in their cistern.
9. A. Thorley, personal communication.

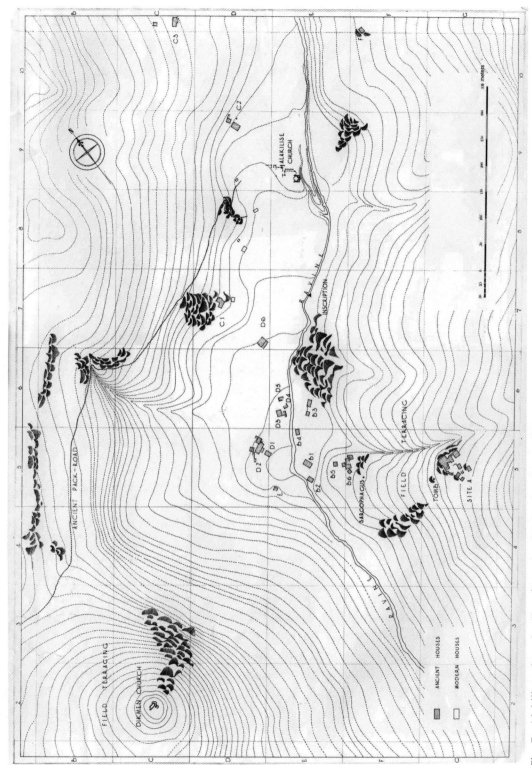

Fig. 7. Alakilise; plan of valley. (Drawing by Gordon Lawson.)

Fig. 8. Alakilise valley; traditional granary. (Drawing by Gordon
Lawson.)

terraces in the valley for wheat growing, and two fig trees and several olives
of great age may be descended from much earlier cultivation. There are also
two or three grapevines, which may be survivors from the vineyards that
probably occupied the extensive terracing on the valley slopes. The extent of
the terracing was impossible to record precisely, because of the undergrowth
on the densely wooded hillsides. However, it could be traced over many
hectares on the northern and northwestern slopes of the valley. These slopes
have an angle as steep as forty degrees, and the terrace walls, which follow
the contours, are often over a meter high.

The most conspicuous building at Alakilise is a church of late fifth- or early
sixth-century date, which was largely rebuilt in May 812 and at that time
dedicated to the archangel Gabriel (fig. 48). It was discovered by an Austrian
expedition under Petersen and von Luschan in 1882 and studied again by
Rott in 1906.[10] The plan is a basilica with a cross-in-square chapel (evidently

10. Petersen and von Luschan 1889, 38–40; Rott 1908, 318–24.

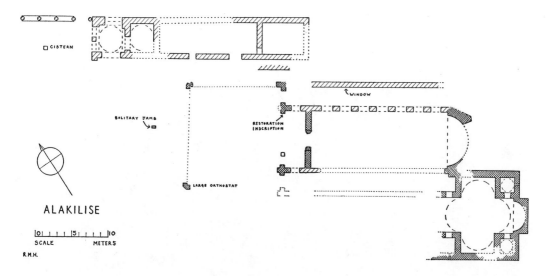

Fig. 9. Alakilise; church complex of the archangel Gabriel, plan

an addition) south of the apse and includes various outbuildings (figs. 9–10, 47). There were two main periods of construction. Originally, the church had columns in the nave and rich sculpture, especially capitals, cornices, pilasters, and jambs (figs. 11–16, 49). The ninth-century rebuilding followed in general the original plan. The church had the same apse and much of the narthex, but the new north wall of the nave consisted of two superimposed arcades, and a gallery was placed above the north aisle. There were at least three later periods of modification and contraction. The last is represented by the walling up of the northern gallery arcade when that gallery had for some reason fallen into disuse. The church probably remained in use until the eleventh or twelfth century.[11]

Sculpture from the early Christian period included several local limestone capitals. One example was of Ionic type, richly decorated with acanthus and large rosettes, and at least two pier capitals were found, with windblown acanthus, crosses, and six-point stars. Other sculptures included architraves, jambs, and a puteal.[12] These pieces are carefully carved, as are those from Muskar (figs. 40–43, 96).[13] On the western end of the church is a sculptured cornice with extremely rich decoration. This is not an isolated example, as there are similarly decorated churches inland, both on Alaca

---

11. Harrison 1963, 125–29, 145–46, pls. XXXVIa–d, XXXVIIa–c; 1977, 11; 1980, 116, pl. XXV.
12. Harrison 1972, 188–93.
13. Harrison 1963, 131, 146, pl. XXXVIe; 1972, 192–95. See also section on Muskar church earlier in this chapter.

Fig. 10. Alakilise; church complex of the archangel Gabriel, northeast
chamber and apse

Fig. 11. Alakilise; church complex of the archangel Gabriel, stone
screen with peacocks flanking cross (half-scale; found in south aisle area
of church; scale 1/2: the frame is cut back approximately 0.04 m, the
birds and cross are approximately 0.01 m in relief and the block is 0.15
m thick)

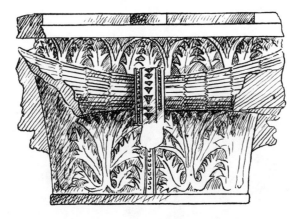

Fig. 12. Alakilise; church complex of the archangel Gabriel, detail of capital

Fig. 13. Alakilise; church complex of the archangel Gabriel, capital

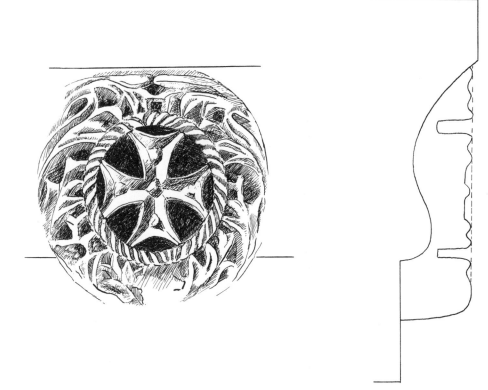

Fig. 14. Alakilise; church complex of the archangel Gabriel, pilaster capital (scale 1/2)

Fig. 15. Alakilise; church complex of the archangel Gabriel, detail of north jamb of doorway from narthex to nave

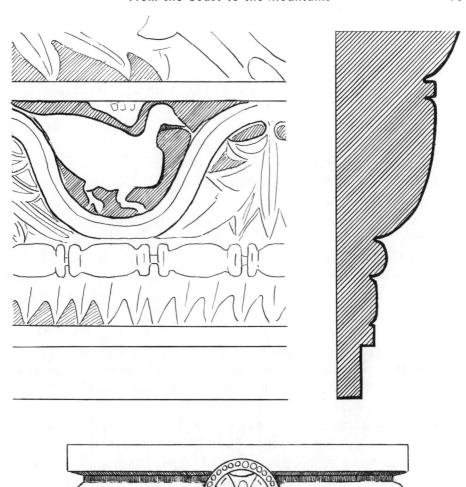

Fig. 16.   Alakilise; church complex of the archangel Gabriel,
decorative details (bird: scale 1/2; capital: scale 1/5)

Dağ (Alacahisar [figs. 28–29, 93], Devekuyusu [figs. 25–26, 63], Dikmen
[figs. 21, 54–55], and Karabel-Asarcık [figs. 23–24, 58–61])[14] and around
Elmalı (Tekkeköy [fig. 77], Müğren [fig. 78], Serkiz Alanı, and Ovacık).[15]
   However, apart from one or two sculptured pieces from Limyra and

14. Harrison 1960b, 305; 1963, 130–37, 146–48. See also descriptions later in this chapter.
15. For Tekkeköy, see Harrison 1972, 196, fig. 20. For Müğren, see Harrison 1980, 110, pl. XIXa.
For Serkiz Alanı, see Harrison 1984, figs. 6–7. For Ovacık, see Harrison 1980, 110 n. 6. See also chap. 3
below.

perhaps Myra,[16] nothing similar has been found from the coast. The Lycians had a long tradition of good stonework. We may infer, therefore, that there took place a geographical switch of wealth and patronage away from the coastal cities, in which the best craftsmen were attracted up to these inland settlements. There were still settlements on the coast, but their populations had generally declined. However, the villages and monasteries inland seem to have been comparatively rich in late antiquity.

Even more interesting than the church was a large ancient village at the head of the valley, with both terraced and freestanding houses (fig. 7).[17] There is evidence that a large area had been opened up by forest clearance and that the timber thus obtained was used for house building. A group of over forty stone-built houses was recorded, with walls generally standing to their full height of two storys.

The largest complex, site A, terraced into the eastern hillside, consists of at least five terraces, each of two-story buildings, apparently extending more than one hundred meters along the slope (fig. 50). The lower story is entered from one level, the upper story from the terrace above. The windows are arched, and the doorways have good thresholds and lintels; the walls are 0.70 meters thick and contain recesses that were presumably cupboards. In the floor of the entrance court is a bell-shaped cistern. The upper floors and roofs were presumably of timber.

The detached houses are more typical, and most had two rooms on each of two storys, with walls between 0.60 and 0.80 meters thick.

House B2, which stands beside a small ravine, has a southern doorway, rabbets for the upper floor, and windows apparently only in the upper story. The smaller room is 6.4 meters wide, 3.23 meters long; the larger room 6.31 meters wide, 5.25 meters long. The ground floor was probably used for storage or to house animals.

B1 is a similar house nearby; again it has upper windows (some of which had been blocked), and there is an arched recess in the outer wall, above an external bell-shaped cistern. The house consists of one long room, measuring 10.35 by 14.05 meters (fig. 17).

A third house (B3) has a northern doorway, outside which lies a rough column. It is two-storied, with a yard, and its rectangular room measures 4.84 by 5.55 meters. Again there are no windows in the lower story. To the north, 9.28 meters away, is a two-roomed building, with external and inter-

---

16. For Limyra, see Borchhardt 1974, 40–41; 1975a, 34. For Myra, see Harrison 1972, 195–96, fig. 19.

17. Harrison 1978, 335–37; 1979a, 528–29, pls. 5–8, fig. 2; 1979b, 228, figs. 3–4; 1980, 116–18, pls. XXIII, XXIVb–XXIXa.

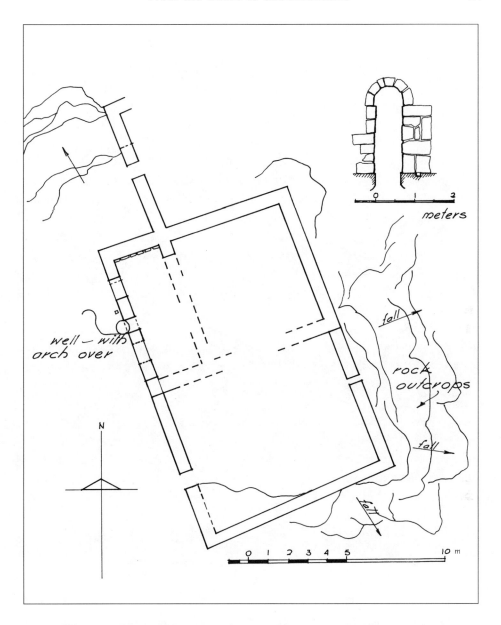

Fig. 17. Alakilise valley; house B1 plan. (Drawing by Gordon Lawson.)

nal doorways. The two rooms are 5.65 meters wide and about 10 meters long.

C1 (a terraced building) lies on a slope (figs. 18, 51). It has two rooms at the lower level and various annexes above, with a high-level courtyard 8.75 meters long to the rear. The yard contains a plaster-lined rock-cut cistern

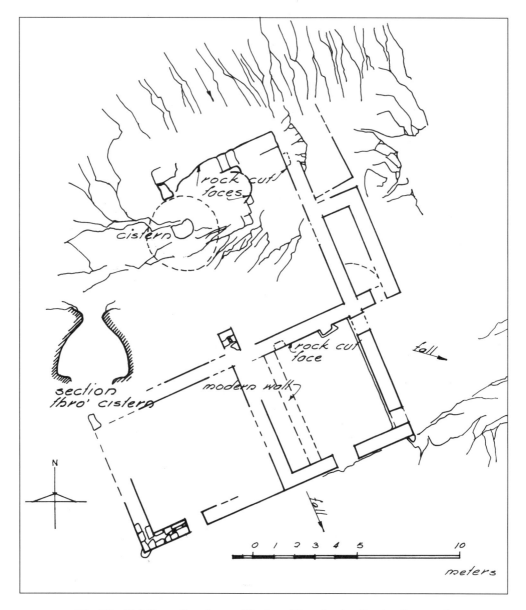

Fig. 18. Alakilise valley; house C1 plan. (Drawing by Gordon Lawson.)

(2.8 m deep, 2/3.6 m wide internally) and a niche in the rock to take the beam for a winepress. Rocky outcrops surround the house and also occur in the yard. One upper room contains a possible fireplace. A small room outside may have housed a dog or other animals. The south room measures 7.47 meters long by 6.89 meters wide, with an entrance 0.94 meters wide; the north room is 6.83 meters long and 6.89 meters wide, with an entrance 1.10 meters wide. The area is on the edge of the snow line in winter.

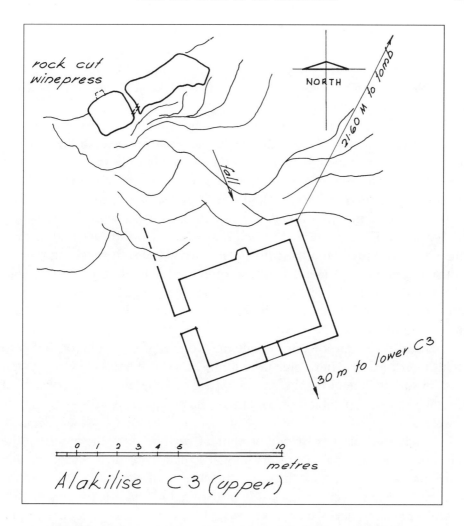

Fig. 19. Alakilise valley; house C3 (upper) plan. (Drawing by Gordon Lawson.)

House C2 has two rooms, of which the westernmost is 8.06 meters wide externally and 7.60 meters wide internally. Another house lies 6.75 meters away, consisting of one square room and two narrower rooms, 15.30 meters long and 10.08 meters wide. The latter each have a narrow entrance and two additional windows.

The two rooms of House C3 are 17.85 meters long, and each room has an entrance. The area outside is rocky and contains a cistern.

Site C3 upper affords a particularly good example of a rock-cut winepress. The upper rectangular pressing floor is about two meters square and leads by pierced spout into a deep circular trough, which is about one meter in diameter, and both are plaster-lined (fig. 19).

The gorge presumably used to be dry in summer then as now, for each house had its own well. There is also a rock-cut inscription of classical date in the lower part of the gorge, which suggests that its position was easily accessible and within view during at least part of the year, presumably when the river was not flowing.

There are probably up to one hundred houses in the village — some to the north of our plan, and some to the south — and many houses in the planned area were not examined. The population was likely to have been over five hundred. The village was scattered, but the houses were similar in type, and there was no apparent development of style. The date is in late antiquity, probably sixth century, although the church itself was restored in the early ninth century. Each house had its bell-shaped cistern, and each had its rectangular or oval press and its trough. This would seem to suggest a regular industry, and the area may have been organized deliberately as an agricultural village supplying the city of Myra. The church of St. Gabriel itself had three underground cisterns, one in the narthex, one in the northwest corner, and one to the south.

There is evidence not only about the lives of the population but also about their burials. There are three tombs, one of them lying close to the cross-in-square chapel on the southwest side of the church. It consists of several fragments of gabled sarcophagus (the end gable is 0.38 m high, 0.91 m wide).

Beside house complex B6 and prominently overlooking the mouth of the valley is a fine sarcophagus of traditional Lycian type. It is placed exactly east-west. A Latin cross is incised at each end of the lid, and a cross is inscribed within a circle on each side of the lid. On one side of the trough is incised a *tabula ansata,* which, however, is blank. The crosses, *tabula ansata,* and other decorations are carefully cut in identical technique and are thought to be primary. The length of the lid (without bosses) is 2.15 meters; its height is 0.70 meters. The height of the Latin cross on each end of the lid is 0.53 meters; the diameter of the compass-drawn cross on each side of the lid is 0.48 meters. The *tabula ansata* is 0.89 × 0.35 meters in size.[18]

The third tomb is a large ossuary, rock-cut and used for multiple burials. A prominent outcrop of rock, externally amorphous, was carefully hollowed out from above to provide a capacious chamber in the form of an oblong truncated pyramid, 2.60 meters long by 1.80 meters wide internally. This chamber is sealed by a lid of debased Lycian type, 2.48 meters long, about 1.60 meters high, and flattened but with the telltale hog's-back spine.

---

18. Harrison 1979b, 229; 1980, 117, pl. XXX.

Four knobs pierced for suspension should perhaps have been removed after the lid was lowered into place. A carefully cut rectangular opening 0.45 meters high and 0.52 meters wide at the eastern end of the rock, which was 0.43 meters thick at this point, provided access for secondary and subsequent burials.[19] The shape of the tomb closely resembles a Turkish nomad's tent. All three tombs seem to have been about fifth century in date.

The agricultural terraces are long and narrow. Those in the valley were presumably for wheat growing, while those on the western, northern, and eastern slopes were probably for grapevines. Examples of similar terraces also occur around Karabel-Asarcık (see the relevant section later in this chapter). Sion (probably modern Karabel) is mentioned in texts in connection with grape growing and also wine production. There are good references for grapevines being grown in this area in the sixth century, particularly in the *Life of St. Nicholas of Sion*.[20] However, the large-scale cultivation of olive trees is less likely because of the height of the valley and the possibility of winter frosts. Perhaps the trees on the slopes were cut down to make the terraces but eventually grew again, after cultivation ceased. The many plants and lichens found at Dikmen near Alakilise help to confirm this possibility.[21] It was a rich site, but perhaps it was overdeveloped. The felling of the trees and subsequent loosening of the soil would have allowed the soil to be washed down the gorge by the river to Myra, and this could have been a contributory factor toward the deposition of alluvium there.

There are further ancient sites within a kilometer to the east, north, southwest, and south of Alakilise. To the east, on the slopes of Alaca Dağ about a kilometer away, is another small ancient settlement, with two chapels, several houses, and at least nine cisterns. To the north, on the steep western slope at Saraylı half a kilometer away, is a partly rock-cut and partly ashlar chapel. A short flight of steps leads up to an arched doorway in the wall built across the front of the cell; the masonry is carefully cut ashlar, and the wall is also pierced by an arched window. The length, breadth, and height of the chamber are each about three meters. Inside, the north wall is decorated with a huge Latin cross in high relief (1.63 m tall, with the background cut to 0.20 m), a semicircular niche, and two rows of compass-drawn crosses. Above the chapel, on the rock face, are carved a small peacock (0.15 m long), a cross formed of two twisted loops, and a Latin cross with a tiny cord-encircled Maltese cross at its center (figs. 20, 52). Adjoining the chapel to the north is a rock-cut apsidal recess decorated with a compass-drawn Maltese

19. Harrison 1979b, 229; 1980, 117–18, pl. XXIXb.
20. Ševčenko and Ševčenko 1984, 96–97.
21. A. Thorley, personal communication.

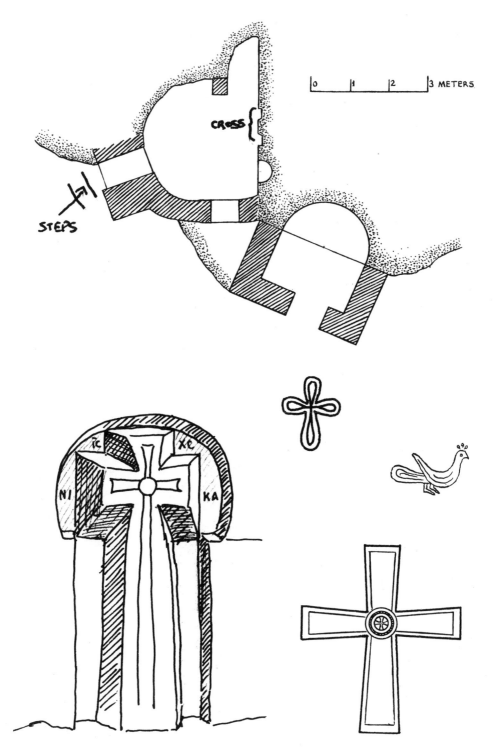

Fig. 20. Alakilise valley; rock-cut chapels at Saraylı, 1 km north of main church (details: the smallest cross measures ca. 0.15 m high; bird measures ca. 0.15 m long; second small cross measures ca. 0.90 m high)

cross and surmounted by slanting grooves for a pitched roof; this roof had extended out from the rock about two meters, over a rectangular enclosure of rough walling with a doorway. Another small rock-cut chamber (with a cistern beneath its floor, fed from the wall by a terra-cotta pipe) lies fifty meters south of the chapel; near it is a shallow grave, cut in the vertical rock face. The date of the complex is about ninth or tenth century.[22]

Dikmen

At Dikmen, southwest of Alakilise, about twelve hundred meters above sea level, and above the road to Muskar, there is a *triconchos* church of the sixth century (fig. 21). It is built of fine large ashlar, but only the southern apse stands above the lowest courses (figs. 54–55). In this apse is a doorway leading to an adjoining chapel and surmounted by an imposing lintel with curved inner face. The chord of the eastern apse is about 4.50 meters, and the outer faces of the three apses were probably rectangular; that of the southern certainly was. Although the standing doorway belongs to the original building, the side chapel appears to have been added later; there is no bond, and its masonry is markedly inferior. A small chapel 15 meters long and 5.70 meters wide was built within the main church, at a later date, comprising an antechamber, single nave, and apse. The masonry was stone-faced rubble, with liberal use of mortar and tile fragments, and several well-cut voussoirs of the first period are built into the walls. The church has a view down to Alakilise and the coast (fig. 53).[23]

Below Alakilise, the valley narrows to a gorge. Here, a chapel and houses of similar type to those at Alakilise were situated on a very small patch of level ground.[24] There was obviously a considerable population in the valley in late antiquity. The gorge becomes increasingly steep as it descends, but a path does exist leading down to Myra (Demre). It is extremely steep and rocky (identified in Turkish as *boş merkep yol,* "empty donkey road"), and it is easy to understand why another ancient (and modern) path climbs up the side of the valley and over to Muskar before descending to Myra (fig. 45).

Turant Dağ

The lower section of the valley is dominated on the west by Turant Dağ, a steep tabletop mountain about 850 meters high, which overlooks the Myra

---

22. Petersen and von Luschan 1889, 40; Harrison 1963, 129; Harrison 1979b, 229, fig. 5.
23. Harrison 1960b, 305; 1963, 130–31, fig. 8, pl. XXXVIId.
24. Harrison 1979b, 229, 232.

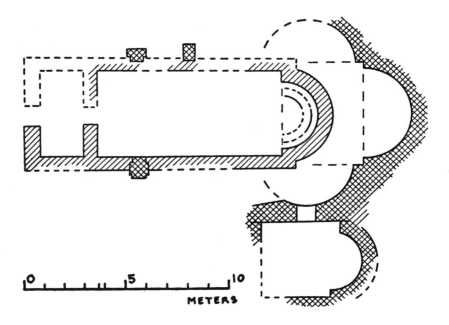

Fig. 21. Dikmen; plan of church

plain. In this area is an extensive Roman necropolis, and other buildings include a substantial late Roman vaulted structure, which may be a bathhouse, and the remains of a large church of fine ashlar, evidently of the sixth century (figs. 22, 56).[25] This church also was *triconchos* in plan, without a narthex, and a small chapel was constructed inside it at a later date. There is some sculpture (including a cross with the Greek letter rho in a circular wreath, topped by a small star), large ashlar masonry on the apse and the south baptistery, a font, and a collapsed sculptured console, which recalls similar features at Karabel-Asarcık (about three hours away on foot). That church is also sixth century in date and *triconchos* in plan, with a baptistery and a funerary chapel, and with eight consoles arranged around the inner wall of the apse, probably to support lamps.

There are many questions to ask about Alakilise. Were church and village contemporary, or did one precede the other? Did both church and village have continued occupation right through from the sixth century until the ninth century and later? Why did the settlement have a heyday in the sixth century and another (for the church at least) in the ninth century? Was the settlement set up solely for agricultural purposes to supply Myra but not to trade elsewhere? How important was the practice of seasonal migration

25. Ibid., 232, figs. 6–7.

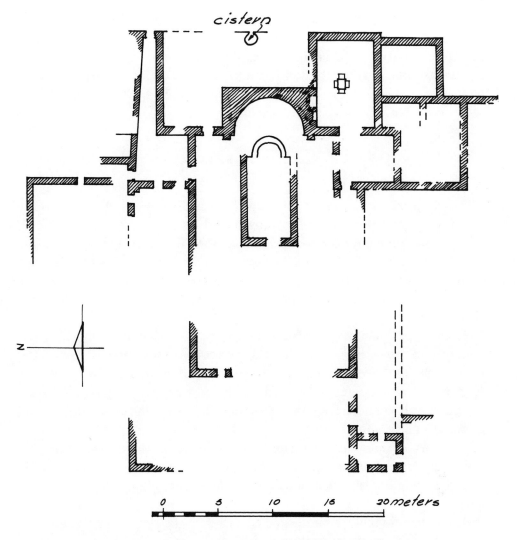

Fig. 22. Turant Dağ; plan of church complex. (Drawing by Gordon Lawson.)

inland from the coast? Two references may suggest a history of seasonal migration in Lycia. One is from the sixth century B.C. at Xanthos, when Herodotus reported that eighty families escaped massacre by the Persians; George Bean believed that they were probably away at their *yayla* (upland pastures).[26] The second reference concerns Myra in 1087, when merchants from Bari visited the city in search of the relics of St. Nicholas; they found that the population had disappeared into the hills.[27] There are similar

26. Herodotus *Historiae* I.176; Bean 1978, 50.
27. Ševčenko 1983, 23 n. 35.

examples in Pamphylia.[28] In the seventh century and later, Arab attacks
were certainly a problem on the coast. Was malaria also a factor? How
much did environmental changes (e.g., the silting up of the land or the loss
of water supplies) affect the settlements? How far is this pattern, whatever
its causes, repeated along the coast of Asia Minor? In Pisidia the picture
seems different, but Isauria may be similar to Lycia.

Karabel-Asarcık

A modern track from Muskar climbs to a small ancient and modern village
called Karabel, on the mountain ridge between Myra and Arneae. To the
north is a small walled settlement now called Asarcık. The site of Karabel-
Asarcık is a commanding one, with fine views to the north and west over the
Kasaba valley (figs. 57, 97) and also to the south, where the sea may be seen
on the horizon above the forest. An ancient road led from Myra to Karabel
via Muskar, and another route from that village came to the site via
Devekuyusu.

The very fragmentary remains of a basilica with single projecting apse can
be traced in the modern hamlet. At the northwest and southwest corners of
the church are the foundations of two circular structures (towers?), three to
four meters in diameter. Appended to the east end of the south aisle is a
curious barrel-vaulted chamber. Its north wall follows the curve of the apse;
its south wall contains its only door.[29]

Two further churches lie on the mountain ridge, the upper within the
walled settlement and the lower (and larger) outside the wall. The former
has rich sculpture and may have been a monastery, as, indeed, may the
latter.

The upper church is a basilica constructed on the summit of an acropolis
fortified by high walls of massive boulders (fig. 62). The church was 18.80
meters long excluding a single projecting apse (with the chord measuring
4.90 m); there are traces of windows (0.90 m wide) in the east ends of
the two aisles, and the west wall had three doors; evidently there was no
narthex. There is rich sculpture, which may be slightly earlier than the
church.[30]

The second and larger church lies outside the walls and below the acropolis (figs. 23, 58).[31] The nave was about twenty-eight meters long including a

---

28. De Planhol 1958, 234–39.
29. Harrison 1963, 131.
30. Ibid., 136.
31. For a comprehensive survey of this site, see Harrison 1963, 131–35, 146–47, pls. XXXVIII–
XLII. See also Harrison 1960a, 26–28; Harrison 1960b, 305–6; Harrison 1961, 6–7; Harrison 1972, 197,
fig. 24; Harrison 1977, 11, 14; Severin 1977, 23; Grossman and Severin 1981, 101–10.

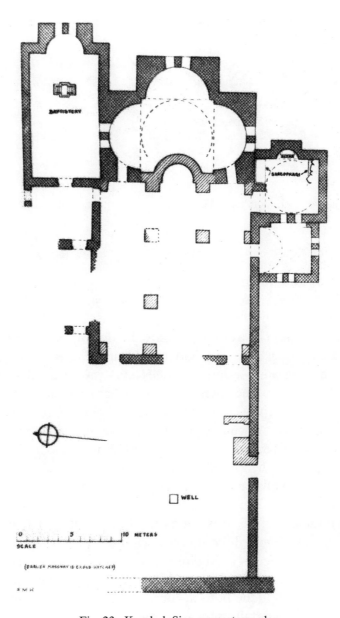

Fig. 23. Karabel; Sion monastery, plan

triconchos (i.e., trefoil or cloverleaf) sanctuary, the three apses being externally rectangular and about eight meters wide (fig. 59). The internal chord of the apses measured 6.20 meters. The side aisles terminate in barrel-vaulted passages leading into the north and south apses, respectively; another doorway in the north apse gives access to the adjoining baptistery, which had a cruciform font. Three doorways at the west end of the church

Fig. 24. Karabel; Sion monastery, cornice fragment lying in domed mortuary chapel

open onto an atrium about twenty meters long; there is no narthex. The masonry is laid in two faces of accurately cut, carefully finished blocks, often of imposing dimensions.

Each of the apses is lit by a double window divided by a small pillar. On the double voussoir above is a cross in sharp relief, and the cross in the south apse is formed by a monogram inscription of ZωH and ΦωC, flanked by the letters A and Ω in relief. Around the apses runs an enriched cornice. At the center of each apse, over the cornice, is a *tabula ansata* in relief outline beneath the bottom of a large cross, which must originally have reached the crown of the apse. The *tabula ansata* and the cross have a pitted surface as if to take plaster and possibly mosaic. The church may have had a central dome on pendentives, and it probably dates to the early sixth century.

Flanking the south aisle of the church and accessible from it are two chapels, of which the easternmost is the earlier (figs. 60–61). The masonry in this eastern chapel is fine ashlar, and the sculpture includes two extraordinarily rich cornices (fig. 24). Rudimentary pendentives support a heavy dome, in which there is a cross-shaped window. A puzzling feature of the chapel is the insertion, in the bottom course of the dome, of eight regularly spaced consoles of uncertain purpose, although a reasonable explanation might be that a lamp was suspended from each. The chapel contains three broken sarcophagi and a small altar with a cross.

This church is extremely important from the architectural point of view. A problem current in the sixth century was how to fit the elevation of a dome on the square plan of a nave. There were interesting developments in the late fifth century in Isauria. For example, at the site of Alahan,[32]

32. Bakker 1985, 112–13, pl. 33.

squinches were used to place an octagonal domelike tower on the nave. The church of St. Sophia in Constantinople had an oblong nave and a circular dome on pendentives.[33] At an earlier date, there was perhaps a dome on the church of St. Polyeuktos, built in the 520s.[34] The *triconchos* churches with domes on pendentives in Lycia are contemporary, but they are both developed from fifth-century examples in Isauria.[35] The architect of the Sion monastery (see the discussion that follows) was, incidentally, named Konon, which is a common name in Isauria.[36]

Several aspects of this church need consideration. These include the date of the initial building, the approximate date of various modifications in the main body of the church, the possibility of a gap in occupation between these dates, the existence of a previous settlement before the sixth century, and the identification of the site with the monastery of Sion. The location of this monastery is an extraordinarily interesting subject.

In 1963 it was proposed that the lower church of Karabel-Asarcık was probably the monastery of Nicholas of Sion.[37] Nicholas was archimandrite (abbot) and built the monastery; later he became bishop of Pinara and finally returned to die at Sion. The *Life of St. Nicholas of Sion* is contemporary, probably written by one of the monks of his monastery soon after Nicholas's death. The text was published by Gustav Anrich in 1913.[38] Another text, with translation and comments by Ihor and Nancy Ševčenko, was published in 1984.[39] The *Life* contains important material concerning the history of the region at this time. For example, the account states that Nicholas traveled to Palestine three times (once via Egypt), and the descriptions of these journeys throw valuable light on Lycia's maritime contacts. There are about thirty-five named places (mostly villages and monasteries) in Lycia itself, but as yet we only know the locations of Myra, Andriake, Arneae, Phoinix, Akalissus, Chelidon and Tristomon (which is now called Üçağız), and it is hoped that inscriptions may one day be found that will enable these names to be ascribed to particular sites. The miracles described are instructive. They include the discovery and purification of wells (water was always scarce) and the miraculous felling of a demon-ridden tree (plausibly identified with the end of a pagan cult).

In accordance with the law at that time, episcopal permission to build the

---

33. Mainstone 1988, 37.
34. Harrison 1989b, 131.
35. Hill 1979, 9.
36. Mango 1966, 363 n. 20.
37. Harrison 1960a, 26–28; 1960b, 305–6; 1961, 6–7.
38. Anrich 1913–17; cf. Robert 1955, 197–208.
39. Ševčenko and Ševčenko 1984.

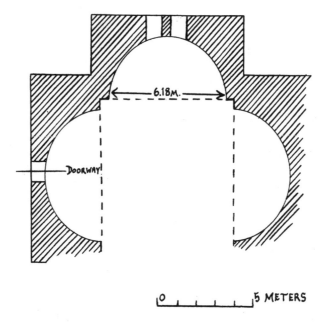

Fig. 25. Devekuyusu; plan of apse of church

Sion monastery had been requested, and the site was approved by the archbishop of Myra. Relations with the succeeding archbishop, however, were
not so smooth. An outbreak of the plague at Myra was followed by famine,
and the archbishop complained to the civil authorities that Nicholas Sionites
was not allowing the farmers to bring down to the city grain or flour, wine or
wood, or anything else needed for subsistence. He tried to have Nicholas
arrested.

However, soon afterward Nicholas consolidated his position in the countryside. He toured the villages and monasteries of the valleys and the hilltops. At
each place, he sacrificed two or more bullocks, which he purchased locally,
and fed the people on the meat. He also gave them bread and wine, which he
brought from the Sion monastery. He covered ten villages in twenty days in
this way, presumably using pack animals. The villages must have included
Muskar, Alakilise, and Turant.

The ancient road from Myra to Karabel continued northward through
Çağman, where there was a church that appeared however to be considerably later than sixth century in date.[40] There was presumably also a
track to the city of Arneae to the northwest, and then the road probably
ran northeastwards, crossing the route from Finike to the Elmalı plain, to

---

40. Harrison 1963, 137.

Stone block 0.245 X 0.06 X 0.04 m.

Fig. 26. Devekuyusu; sketch of sculpture (the stone block is 0.245 ×
0.06 × 0.04 m)

Arykanda and eventually Akalissus and Edebessos. The ancient site of
Edebessos has a sixth-century church and Roman sarcophagi,[41] and Akalissus, in an area which is steep and wooded, was the site of the monastery
of Nicholas's uncle. Nicholas is known to have traveled from Sion to
Akalissus.[42]

Anrich set out reasons (from internal evidence in the *Life*) for locating
the site of Sion on the west side of Alaca Dağ, equally accessible from Myra
and Arneae. The church was built on a hillside, but the plan was multi-
apsed, and the building blocks were so large that divine assistance was
claimed for their erection. Nicholas's tomb was on the south side of his
church, where there were also the relics of various martyrs; if it is rightly
identified, this would explain the domed chapel. The location is right, as is
the date (which preceded the plague in 542).

There are three very similar *triconchos* churches in the area: one at
Devekuyusu, north of Muskar and east from Karabel toward Alakilise (figs.
25–27, 63);[43] a second at Dikmen, near Alakilise (figs. 21, 54–55);[44] and a
third at Alacahisar, three kilometers southwest of Karabel (figs. 28–29, 64–
66, 93).[45]

41. Spratt and Forbes 1847, 1:168–70; Bean 1978, 139–40.
42. Spratt and Forbes 1847, 1:167–68; Bean 1978, 140; Ševčenko and Ševčenko 1984, 22–23, 86–87.
43. Harrison 1960b, 305; Harrison 1963, 137, 148; Severin 1977, 24; Harrison 1980, pl. XVIIIb.
44. Harrison 1960b, 305; 1963, 130–31, fig. 8, pl. XXXVIId. See also section on Dikmen in present
chapter, above.
45. Harrison 1960b, 305; 1963, 136, 147–48, pl. XLIII.

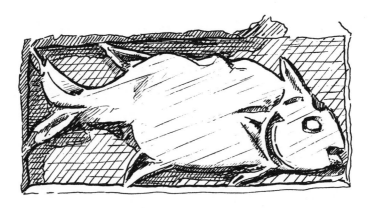

Fig. 27. Carving of fish (said to come from Devekuyusu)

Devekuyusu

The body of the church at Devekuyusu has vanished, but its *triconchos* sanctuary is pierced by one double window in the eastern apse and by another in the northern apse, above a doorway (fig. 25). Two courses of the semidome of the eastern apse remain in situ above a plain cornice (fig. 63). The dimensions of the *triconchos* sanctuary (the chord of the apse measures 6.20 m) approximate very closely to that at Karabel, but the ashlar masonry is neither so massive nor so carefully dressed. The small pillar dividing the eastern window is decorated in relief with a Latin cross above an orb, and a small fragment of acanthus-scroll carving, found among fallen masonry in the sanctuary, resembles closely in style a piece from Alacahisar.

Alacahisar

The eastern half of the church at Alacahisar is cut from the rock in faithful imitation of ashlar stone, and the imitation also extends to the exterior (figs. 28, 29, 64, 93). The crowns of the apses and of the main arch (which was of masonry) are linked by fully developed pendentives, which provide the circular basis for a central dome. At one point, the rock rises 0.75 centimeters above the rim, and the dome was probably finished in light masonry. There is good quality sculpture on the pilasters, jambs, and lintel (figs. 65, 66), which can be dated to the sixth century or perhaps a little later. The Alacahisar church is similar to that at Karabel, but the ashlar church came first and the rock-cut church second. This is surely evidence of the preeminence of the Karabel monastery. It seems that the lower church of Karabel-

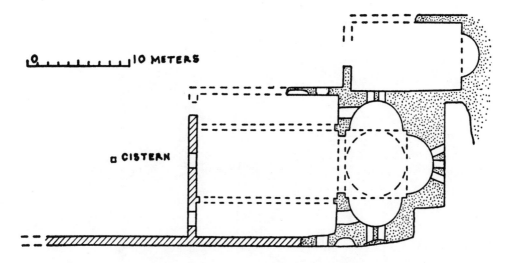

Fig. 28. Alacahisar; plan of rock-cut church

Asarcık, with its commanding situation, its multitude of subchapels, its high-quality masonry and exquisite carving, and with the church at Alacahisar built in imitation, is the most likely site for the Sion monastery of St. Nicholas.

Kumluca Hoard

In August 1963 a very large hoard of early Byzantine liturgical silver, deliberately crushed and buried, came to light at Kumluca near Finike.[46] The hoard consisted of over a hundred major pieces, including six patens, four chalices, two bowls, half a dozen book covers, a dozen *polycandela* (candelabra), a dozen lamps, revetments and sheathings, and much more. The silver was decorated with gilt and niello, and the total weight of the collection must have amounted to several hundredweights. The control stamps date the silver to A.D. 550–65, the late Justinianic period. This hoard is at present split between the Antalya Museum in Turkey and Dumbarton Oaks in the United States. Several items are inscribed with the name of Sion. Myra had been sacked by a naval expedition of Haroun-el-Raschid in 809, and it is conjectured that these tough Arabs may have reached both Karabel and Alakilise (each about four hours' hard trudge from the coast) and that the treasure, if stolen from Karabel, was buried at this time.

46. Fıratlı 1965, 523–25; Dumbarton Oaks 1967, 18–20; Harrison 1977, 14.

Fig. 29. Alacahisar; sketch of apse of church

The track from Karabel to Finike is an obvious escape route across the mountains, leading down to the Finike plain and Kumluca.[47] It is possible that the silver treasure was taken by the Arabs, who for some reason buried it, presumably as a temporary measure, before embarking from the nearby port. This seems to be a much more reasonable explanation of its presence in Kumluca than any suggestion that Kumluca was the site of the Sion monastery.

Arykanda-Arif

A good modern road follows the line of an ancient one that climbed from the Elmalı plain at eleven hundred meters above sea level to the Avlanbeli pass a hundred meters higher, where there are cedars of Lebanon, and descended

47. In this context it is interesting to note that when we were staying at Alakilise, a local shepherd called Süleyman went each Thursday directly to the mosque at Finike using this track and returned on Friday evening. The silver is extremely heavy, but when I traveled for some months in the mountains with a donkey, we could easily carry fifty kilograms or a hundredweight, and we could probably have taken much more.

thence through pinewoods to the orange groves of the coast, along the valley of the Arycandus (modern Aykırıçay) River (fig. 67). Here is limestone country, and the waters of the Elmalı plain, having disappeared into sink-holes, reemerge in abundance from the cliffs of Bey Dağ at the modern village of Arif on the eastern side of the valley. The road down to Finike crosses and recrosses the rushing river. Charles Fellows, who ascended the valley on horseback, waxed lyrical: "I know no scenery equal in sublimity and beauty to this part of Lycia. The mere mention of mountain scenery cannot give any idea of the mountains here, which are broken into sections forming cliffs, whose upheaved strata stand erect in peaks many thousand feet high, uniting to form a wild chaos, but each part harmonized by the other; for all is grand, yet lovely. Deep in the ravines dash torrents of the purest water, and over these grow the most luxuriant trees; above are the graver forests of pines upon the grey cliffs, and higher than these are the ranges of mountains capped by snow."[48] Fellows was no stranger to mountain country, for he had pioneered an ascent of Mont Blanc before he came to Lycia.

Arykanda is a classical city that lies to the east of the road from the plateau of Elmalı to Limyra and the coast. The archaeological dating of the city, given by Professor Bayburtluoğlu and his team from Ankara and provided by late Roman coins and other material, extends from the fourth century B.C. to the fifth/sixth century A.D.[49] The city has a theater, agora, odeum, baths, city walls, and a necropolis. A steep aqueduct brought its water supplies from the abundant springs of Bey Dağ, which at 3,086 meters is one of the highest peaks in Lycia. There are vertical cliffs above, and the terrain slopes downhill for about a kilometer to the fast-flowing river. However, at some time in the fifth/sixth century, for various reasons, some of the citizens moved from the original site to a more protected settlement on a promontory, with defensive walls and steep slopes down to the river. Compared with the grandeur of the original city, this was a minor settlement, housing a few hundred people (perhaps only a very few). Perhaps the rest of the population moved — lock, stock, bishop, and barrel — to other new more defensible sites.

The present site, today called Arif (from the name of the modern village nearby), has largely escaped modern notice, as it is concealed by a pinewood. It is an extraordinarily well-preserved subrectangular fortified settlement, approximately 2.5 hectares in size (fig. 30).[50]

---

48. Fellows 1852, 373.
49. Bayburtluoğlu 1976, 98. See also Bayburtluoğlu 1972–92.
50. Harrison 1964, 10; Harrison 1979b, 232–34, figs. 8–11; Harrison 1980, 114–15, pls. XXI–XXII; Harrison and Lawson 1979, 13–17.

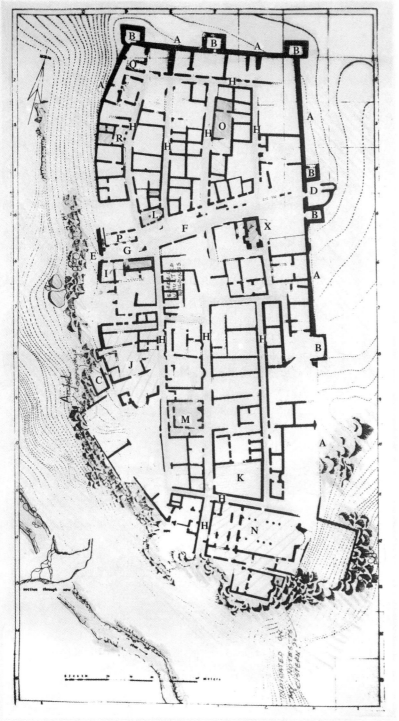

Key

A   curtain wall
B   towers
C   detached tower
D   east gate
E   west gate
F   principal east-west
    street
G   piazza
H   other streets
I   west baths
J   palace
K   open space
    (agora?)
L   chapel (a)
M   church (b)
N   church (c)
    (cathedral?)
O   house (a)
P   house (b)
Q   house (c)
R   house (d)
X   east baths

Fig. 30. Arif; general plan of town. (Drawing by Gordon Lawson.)

Walls and Towers

The town occupies a narrow south-facing promontory, which falls away steeply to the south and west and more gently to the east, to the river some one hundred meters below. It is surrounded on the east, the north, and much of the west by a defensive wall, which on the east and north sides was strengthened by projecting rectangular towers (figs. 69–70, 72). This curtain wall consists of a rough limestone facing with a rubble core and is some 1.75 meters broad. It is standing, in places, to a height of about five meters above present ground level, but the parapet walk is nowhere preserved. There is no wall to the southwest and south, because the steepness of the cliffs renders it unnecessary.

Although the main gate is on the east side, it is evident, from the terrain and from the disposition of the towers, that any attack was expected to come from the north. The towers numbered six, counting clockwise from the northwest corner. There is a detached seventh tower, which may not have been primarily defensive. The east gate was equipped with molded jambs and a lintel that had been salvaged from some Roman monument (fig. 68). This gateway is about 1.82 meters wide and must have been narrower than that of the original Roman building, as there are two sets of door sockets on the lintel's soffit. Outside the gate was built, at a later date, a bow-fronted structure (a tower or possibly a chapel) that was linked by a wall to the south tower of the gate. It would have had the triple effect of concealing the gate, restricting access to it, and confining anyone who did reach it. Towers 4 and 5 guarded the gateway. The lintel of the doorway into tower 5 is visible, and this tower also has the remains of a slit window in both its eastern and southern faces.

The west gate was similarly provided with a reused antique door frame. But here, in view of the very steep drop outside, there were no towers.

The northern city wall remains standing almost to the parapet, at a height of about 4.50 meters. At the northwest corner is an internal staircase or ramp, only about 0.65 meters wide, and there is a similar stairway or ramp immediately north of the west gateway.

The detached seventh tower is well preserved, as its walls are standing to about five meters internally and six meters externally. Its long, oblong platform effectively blocked any extramural circumambulation of the town, as it sits directly over the steep cliffs at the steepest point. In the town wall, an arched doorway (1.47 m wide, with an arch diameter of 1.70 m) leads to the tower (fig. 72).

Streets

The site as a whole was served by a well-organized street system (fig. 71). The principal street runs from the eastern gate to the western and is bordered on its north (sunny) side by an arcade, about five meters wide, which fronted one-room premises (evidently shops), a small church, and the entrances to four subsidiary north-south streets. Eight piers of the arcade are still standing, one to a height of four meters, and two carry the scars of springing voussoirs about three meters wide. There was extensive wall plaster. At its western end, the arcade gave access to a long narrow room with three openings onto a small piazza inside the west gate. In the open area, where the principal street entered the piazza (10 m wide at this end), are the footings of a podium or monument that presumably divided the traffic.

The four subsidiary streets running north from the principal thoroughfare terminate in an east-west street serving the range of large buildings that abut the town's north wall. This is the only lateral street in the northern sector, and it has the effect of dividing the sector into six *insulae,* five running north and the sixth running east-west. Whereas the other streets are approximately straight, the westernmost follows the curve of the town wall, and the easternmost has a large open area on its west side.

Three streets, each about 3.40 meters wide, run south from the principal arcaded street, the central and eastern streets continuing the lines of the eastern pair on the north side, and the western street sitting on a line midway between the westernmost pair to the north. The eastern street toward the northern end is irregular, in that it takes a dogleg to pass two buildings that encroach on it. At the southern end, all three streets open onto an east-west street that runs along the north side of Arif's largest church. The central north-south street continues across this lateral street, past the church's western end, to the cliff face. There are a number of other east-west streets in the southern sector, but they are limited to the width of one block (in one case, possibly two blocks) and thus might better be called passages. There appears to have been only one open area in the southern sector, a trapezoidal court across the street from the north doorway of the large church's atrium. There is evidence that at least part of the western north-south street was roofed over or bridged.

Baths

Two buildings appear to have been baths. Both are on the south side of the principal arcaded street. The first lies southwest of the east gate and is built of uncoursed stones laid in two faces, with hard gray mortar liberally applied. Its walls remain standing to a height of over three meters above ground level. In its eastern section are two adjacent pairs of barrel-vaulted rooms aligned north-south. The interior walls of the two rooms on the eastern side of the building are studded at fairly regular intervals with terra-cotta rods 0.04 meters square. All the rods had been broken off except one in the east wall of the northeastern room. It seems that these were designed to support a marble revetment, leaving a cavity between facing and wall. There are examples of this elsewhere in Lycia (e.g., at Balboura) and also at Pergamum.[51]

The second bath building lies just inside the west gate on the south side. It featured an elaborate doorway with reused jambs, leading from the street into a western room, which also opened eastward into two more rooms. One of these contained a large fallen fragmentary tympanum (or pediment) 0.83 meters high depicting a lion, presumably taken from a Roman tomb at Arykanda. The mouth of the lion had been pierced to form a waterspout. The inner wall of the other room had a system of rectangular terra-cotta bars similar to that in the eastern baths.

If these buildings were indeed baths (as seems most probable), they were presumably public baths, as may be inferred from their position on a main street. There is no trace of the aqueduct that must have served them. More-over, a large tripartite barrel-vaulted building in the lowest part of the town may have been a cistern.

Palace

A large irregular building with a southern apse in the southwestern part of the town may have been a palace. It is bounded on the east and north by streets (those on the north subsequently blocked up) and on the west by the town wall. An arched doorway in the curtain wall leads to (and is concealed by) a large detached tower that commands a fine view of the valley, and a rock-cut well-like shaft (20 m deep) leads to a natural cave in the cliff face halfway down to the river. There are similar examples of secret exits in, for example, Thrace and Ankara.

Agora

To the north of the largest church or cathedral, is a large trapezoidal open space, flanked by streets on three sides. This may possibly have been an agora.

---

51. Information for Balboura is per J. J. Coulton, personal communication. For Pergamum, see Radt 1980, 514, fig. 17. See also Farrington and Coulton 1990, 55–67.

Churches

There are seven churches or chapels in the settlement, and I here discuss three of them.

A chapel in the northern sector has a single aisle, two doorways flanking an arched window in the southern wall, and another doorway in the west wall. The chapel contained a circular podium 0.70 meters in diameter and 0.69 meters high with moldings, which recalls the Hellenistic fluted drum used as an altar in the basilica at the Xanthos Letöon.[52] Other *spolia* (reused architectural pieces) of Roman date included three fragments of smooth column (0.42 m in diameter) and one fragment of engaged Doric pilaster (0.327 m wide, 0.43 m long, 0.85 m high) with nine flutes, which may just possibly have been part of the *proskenion* (front of the stage) of the theater at Arykanda. North of the building is a narrow room and then an additional very small chapel, with two recessed niches in its north wall.

A second church lies very near the large palatial building. Both faces of the west wall are narrowed by two rabbets that occur above a small arched window. These rabbets were between 0.15 and 0.20 meters wide, reducing the wall core from 0.63 meters to only 0.28 meters. As a street lies immediately to the west of the church, this would appear to indicate an upper room or bridge over the street, for which there may be parallels in Syria. Was there a link between the church and the palace? Architectural fragments in the church included a dozen limestone pieces of decorated cornice, pilaster, and vine-leaf carving. There are fewer pieces, but they are similar to those from Alakilise (figs. 11–16, 49) and Muskar (figs. 40–43, 96), on Alaca Dağ (see mention earlier in this chapter).

A large church occupying the southern tip of the promontory is presumed from its size to have been the cathedral and the seat of the bishop. It is a three-aisled basilica with an externally projecting rectangular apse, forty-four meters in length including the atrium. Piers and pilaster responds show that the nave (8 m wide) was separated from the aisles by nine-arch arcades. To the west lies a small atrium, in which the covered walkway was separated from the central open area by a low wall. Entry to the atrium was from the street to the north or from the street to the west. The three doorways from the atrium to the nave and aisles of the church were framed by molded jambs and lintels of reused stone. The main jambs were each decorated with a sinking for a cross 0.14 meters high, presumably in bronze, with four pinholes for its attachment. The north and west walls of the church still

52. Harrison 1966, 109.

stand up to four meters in height; the north wall of the atrium remains at a height of five meters.

To the west of the cathedral lies a curious oblong room with two entrances but evidently no floor, as the ground drops away inside to the southwest into a rock-cut cavity. The east wall stands to a height of five meters above the hole.

Houses

The majority of the buildings on the site appear to have been private houses with at least two stories and in one case certainly three. Two houses have probable chimneys in the walls of the lower stories; in the three-storied house, an external projection in the uppermost story may have been a flue. (A possible chimney was found in the second story of house C1 at Alakilise [see discussion earlier in this chapter], and there was a definite example on the ground floor of a building at Anemurium in Cilicia.)[53] The stairs and ceilings were probably of timber. There was little evidence to provide information about the roofs, but they were certainly pitched and again probably of timber. I have already mentioned evidence of a link (possibly a bridge) between the church and the possible palace, above the street. Perhaps there were other similar links from house to house.

I here describe four examples of houses at the site.

A building of three stories (standing to about 5 m in height) lies to the northwest of the east gate. It looked down onto a street and a small piazza. In the third story was a wide curved niche supported by two corbels on the western external face. Was this a chimney or maybe a window or lavatory? There are arched windows in the first and second stories.

Another house lies to the north of the west gate. Between it and the town wall (standing here to a height of 4.5 m) is a space of 1.10 meters, into which fitted a stair rising from just inside the west gate to three meters above street level. The building comprised a long narrow room or loggia with three openings onto the piazza, but these openings were later blocked up to form a closed room.

A detached oblong building was found in the northwest corner of the site, with walls standing to a height of 2.5 meters. There are two arched recesses in the south wall and another similar but larger recess in the north wall.

A house to the south of the detached oblong building abuts the town wall

53. Russell 1982, 134.

and has walls standing to a height of three meters. There are three windows looking onto the street. On the south side is an interior niche, which was probably arched; it was well plastered and may have been a fireplace.

A date for the settlement in about the fifth/sixth century seems appropriate. Excavation at Arykanda has shown that there was continuous occupation into the fifth/sixth century but not much later. At Arif, a few pieces of architectural sculpture in one of the basilicas closely resemble sixth-century work at Alaca Dağ. The few identifiable sherds from the site include examples of late Roman African (Hayes's North African type 104c)[54] and Cypriot wares datable to the sixth century and of a local redware found generally on late Roman and early Byzantine sites in Lycia. Moreover, the town plan, although distinctly nonclassical in that it lacks an agora and public monuments, does have an approximately rectangular layout and a broad axial street, which was arcaded on its northern (sunny) side.

Above the town and in the valley below it are broad agricultural terraces. However, so far at least, no other very significant traces of settlement have been found to exist between the head of this long valley and the coastal plain (the territory of Limyra).

Arif would appear to represent the abandonment of a classical site in about the sixth century and the transfer of its greatly reduced population, perhaps fewer than one thousand persons, to a new, tightly packed, defensible but well-organized town nearby. Arif saw little building later than the sixth century. There were few noticeable developments or changes in the town, and it is doubtful whether it lasted much more than a century.[55]

Warren Treadgold, writing on the seventh and early eighth centuries, wrote: "The shrinking of the cities was partly a cause and partly a result of the shrinkage of trade. Even if the original decrease in urban population was the result of plague and invasions, the fact remains that the decreases were not made up once the disasters had passed. As the roads deteriorated, both land and sea travel became less safe, and as the empire's monetary economy was shaken, the countryside sent less food to sustain the cities. Conversely, the shrunken cities needed less food, and had fewer manufactured goods to trade for it. Thus the whole economy shrank. The support that the business of the government, army and Church provided for the cities was no substitute for a vigorous private sector."[56] These comments seem extremely pertinent in the context of Arif-Arykanda.

54. Hayes 1972, 163.
55. Recent discoveries of material around Arif have cast some doubt on this comment.
56. Treadgold 1988, 41–42.

I have examined the village of Alakilise; the churches of Muskar, Alakilise, and Karabel; and the small town at Arif (near Arykanda). In each place, I found buildings of the sixth century and perhaps traces of the early seventh century. But what happened in the Dark Ages? There is evidence of early ninth-century occupation at Alakilise and of a second period of occupation (perhaps in the Dark Ages or possibly later) at Karabel. The church of St. Nicholas at Myra was rebuilt in the eighth or ninth century, and the church at Dereağzı is about ninth century in date. From Xanthos there is some sculpture of the eleventh century. But there is little else.

Chapter 3

The Elmalı Plateau and Its Mountains

This study now moves to the Elmalı plateau and the higher mountains. The modern market town of Elmalı (whose name means "town of apples") lies among orchards and poplar trees, on the northern edge of an upland plateau at a height of eleven hundred meters above sea level. This plateau falls naturally into two plains: the upper, consisting of a valley running northeast; and the lower, which is T-shaped, with a marshy area (Karagöl) immediately southwest of Elmalı, the valley of the Akçay river (flowing east from Gömbe) further to the southwest, and the former Avlan göl (lake) to the south of Elmalı. Modern roads from Burdur and Antalya to the east approach Elmalı via Korkuteli, and main roads lead from Elmalı southward to Finike and Kaş on the coast and also to the northwest, via Güğü Bel and Seki, to the ancient city of Oenoanda and eventually to the river Menderes (Maeander). This last road was formerly neglected and therefore unsuitable for modern car traffic; it surely was there in antiquity. It has now been completely improved.[1]

The two plains, with their lake basins, were formed naturally by alluvium washed down from the hillsides onto the plateau, which had only restricted outlets to the sea. Karagöl, the north lake, was described in 1870 by E. J. Davis, who also commented on the rich wheat fields of the area.[2] The lake also probably produced the leeches that Elmalı sold widely at that period.[3] Surplus water from the Karagöl used to thunder down into the Düden, an impressive cavernous limestone chasm. In the 1960s, the region still had great beauty, and the lakes were full of fish. More recently, they have been completely drained for agricultural purposes, but in any case they were drying out naturally (fig. 73). The Karagöl had a special set of locks with supervision in the 1960s, but now this is barely necessary, because of the irrigation systems

---

1. M. J. Mellink, personal communication.
2. Davis 1874, 237.
3. Spratt and Forbes 1847, 1:286.

48

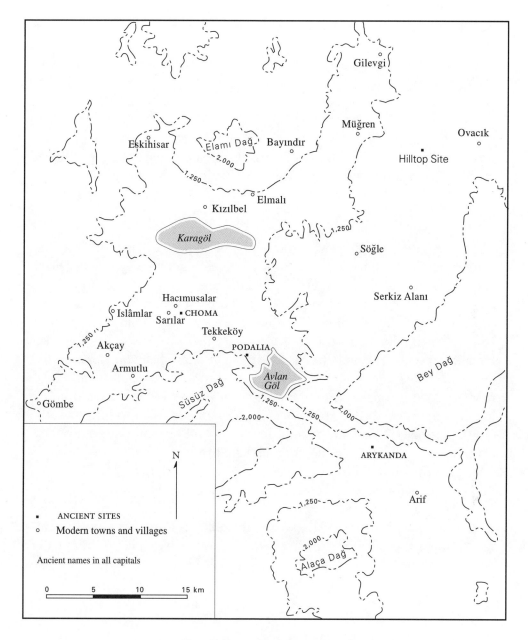

Fig. 31. Map of Elmalı plain and environs

that have been installed. Some thirty years ago there was still some water lying in the lake beds, even in the summer, but now there is only an area of agricultural land, drained by a large canal. The waters of the south lake, the Avlan göl, and of the Akçay River (the ancient Aedesa) were piped underground twenty years ago through the col down to the Arykanda and Arif.

In the past few years, the authorities have developed cedar forests in areas that had previously been bare, particularly in the southern part of the plateau. These areas had probably been cleared of trees during the Roman, medieval, and early modern periods, mainly for timber and firewood.

Choma

There were two Roman towns in the area of Elmalı, Choma and Podalia. Choma has a prehistoric *hüyük* (artificial mound) and lies in the lower plain (fig. 76). It was identified in 1963 by the discovery of a dozen or so inscriptions; some of which are funerary, but one is an honorary decree of the council and people of Choma.[4] The town lies some nine miles southwest of Elmalı, beside the main road to Gömbe and Kaş, which was possibly also the ancient road. The modern Akçay River must have been the same stream as the ancient Aedesa, although its course may have changed slightly. The modern road in this area runs on a low ridge and follows a band a few hundred meters wide of *terra rossa* soils (formed from the residue of weathered limestone). However, to both the north and the south are gray, silty organic soils, belonging to the dried-up lake basins.

A Roman milestone was found at Tekkeköy, a modern village about five kilometers southeast of the site of Choma.[5] It cites "the fourth mile," presumably from Choma, and it would probably have stood on a road leading to Arykanda and the coast. However, Tekkeköy is also about five kilometers from an ancient site at the northwest corner of Avlan göl, traditionally considered to be the second Roman town, Podalia.[6]

Podalia

George Bean proposed that Podalia stood on a hill beside the modern village of Söğle, in the southern foothills of the northeast plateau. He was encouraged by the existence of thick deposits of pottery, including shards

---

4. Harrison 1964, 10; Bean and Harrison 1967, 40–44. Editor's note: Excavations are now taking place near Hacımusalar (the site of ancient Choma) under the direction of Dr. İ Özgen (see supplementary bibliography).

5. Bean and Harrison 1967, 44.

6. Spratt and Forbes 1847, 1:290.

of Hellenistic, Roman, and later dates.[7] There is a cemetery on the summit of the hill, but no other buildings remain. There are, however, several Roman inscriptions and various other carved blocks in the village. Incidentally, the name *Söğle* is not Turkish but belongs, perhaps, to an earlier period, as, for example, that of Sagalassos (a town in Pisidia), whose name is actually pre-Roman.[8]

Despite Bean's suggestions, the Avlan göl site does seem a more likely location for Podalia for various reasons. The original Avlan site is a double hill that produced little material apart from a defensive wall and a tomb.[9] However, the adjacent drained lake bed is very deeply covered with agricultural soil, and large blocks of Roman masonry were visible among the growing wheat when I visited the area. These blocks probably indicate the presence of a substantial settlement, and it could be the site of Podalia.

A chapter in the *Kiborraiots Theme* of Constantine Porphyrogenitus in the tenth century gives two city lists for Lycia.[10] One of them includes the cities of Patara, Xanthos, Myra, Phoinix, and Phaselis on the coast, and the other includes Tlos, Oenoanda, Phileta, and Podalia in the uplands. Radet thought Phileta might be Gilevgi,[11] at the extreme north end of the Elmalı plain, where there is a mound south of the castle, but this identification seems unlikely for two reasons. First, there is no known late Roman or Byzantine pottery from the site, and second, the inland list moves from Tlos to Oenoanda (which are known), eastward to the Elmalı plain, and then into Pisidia. Phileta is the third town, and Podalia is the fourth. If Phileta is Gilevgi, Podalia must be even further outside the plateau, toward Pisidia. But the ancient geographers, for example, Pliny Senior, say that it lay in the plateau.[12] Therefore, Phileta may have been in the center of the plateau or at any rate near to Elmalı.

Kızılbel

Near the Karagöl, at Kızılbel (named for the pass running through an area of striking red soil that leads north to Eskihisar and Seki), is a sixth-century B.C.

7. Bean 1968, 157–63; 1971, 28–32; 1978, 153–56.

8. Editor's note: see supplementary bibliography, Waelkens 1993, 41 n. 42.

9. Petersen and von Luschan 1889, 161–62; Bean 1968, 159–60, fig. 3. Editor's note: The newly discovered *stadiasmos* (an early Imperial monument giving a list of all roads connecting Patara to other towns), as Prof. Sencer Şahin reports, gives the road to Elmalı with separate references to the sites of Podalia and Soklai-Söğle (Prof. Mellink, personal communication to editor; see also supplementary bibliography).

10. Pertusi 1952, 78–79, book XIV, lines 17–22, 35–36.

11. Radet 1893, 188–89.

12. Pliny *Naturalis Historiae* 5.101; Bean 1968, 158 n. 2; Magie 1950, 1372.

tomb excavated by Professor Machteld Mellink, which had rich frescoes depicting a funeral banquet and various other scenes, including depictions of a ship, an important personage with a parasol, and several oarsmen.[13] This site is eighty kilometers from the sea, and the fresco was possibly a lake scene rather than a marine one, if it is not an imaginary depiction. Professor Mellink believes that the paintings in this tumulus depict both lake and sea scenes: there is a hunt in the marshes, where young men in a small boat spear a wild boar, and also a sea voyage, with ample blue waves and a warshiplike well-manned vessel. In the pre-Neolithic period, the Avlan göl was certainly ten meters higher than the modern level, from the evidence of a high-tide mark consisting of a line of flints and shells.

It has been explained that the geography of this area has changed from antiquity to recent times, in particular as the lakes have dried up. The town of Elmalı itself has a prehistoric hüyük and a Turkish site including a Selcuk mosque (fig. 75), but nothing is known of the period between. On the Elmalı plateau are thirty modern villages, in many of which antique pottery has been found, and in six of which (Islâmlar, Müğren, Ovacık, Sarılar, Serkiz Alanı, and Tekkeköy) important ancient sculpture.

Tekkeköy

At Tekkeköy, there is a limestone capital (0.54 m high, with a lower diameter of ca. 0.35 m) with two tiers of windblown acanthus and a third tier of small acanthus leaves set obliquely between volutes (fig. 77). It is certainly of the sixth century and somewhat different from sculpture at Muskar and Alakilise (see chap. 2 and figs. 11–16, 40–43, 49, 96), although showing certain similarities.[14]

Müğren

Another substantial capital was found at Müğren. It also is of limestone and is decorated with windblown acanthus, and on the abacus are two opposed Maltese crosses (fig. 78).[15] It was said to have come from a large building in the eastern sector of the village and was temporarily held in the police house. The capital was taken to Elmalı in 1975 and officially registered (by the Antalya Museum Research Station) in 1988.

The only piece of figured sculpture from early Byzantine Lycia is an

---

13. Mellink 1970, 251–53, pls. 59–61; 1971, 246–55, pls. 50–52.
14. Harrison 1972, 196, fig. 20; cf. 188–95.
15. Harrison 1980, 110, pl. XIXa.

ambo parapet of hard white limestone, which is now in the Antalya Museum but was said to have come from Müğren (fig. 79).[16] The slab, which is oblong, is convex in front, concave behind, and broken vertically, in two approximately equal and joining parts. On each end of the slab is an engaged column, and toward each end of the top surface is a rounded boss. The length of the slab is 1.015 meters (omitting columns), and the height is 0.67/0.70 meters (excluding bosses).

The convex face of the slab is decorated with three figured panels separated by ornamental borders, which consist of undulating plants at either end and lattice pattern on the intermediary vertical borders and the upper border. The figures in the left-hand and right-hand panels are archangels with long wings, dressed in tunics and cloaks. Above the heads of both figures stands a plump bird. The figure in the central panel stands on a small tree with splayed branches. It is wearing a long hooded cloak and stands on tiptoe with upheld palms and rounded eyes and mouth, appearing to exhibit some surprise. Above the hood and within the arch is an encircled Maltese cross, and above the arch are two confronted birds.

The central figure is presumably the Virgin Mary, who is frequently shown standing between angels. What looks like a mustache either is accidental or was added at a later date. If the figure were male, we should expect it to have both mustache and beard. However, as the figure stands on a small tree, it might be supposed to represent a tree demon. I believe that it is certainly female.

This is lively local sculpture. It should certainly postdate the busy period of sculptural activity in the early period of Justinian in Constantinople, and it is probably of late sixth- or early seventh-century date. It is possible to argue, on the basis of this ambo, for the presence of a church where it would have stood and for a settlement that the church served.

An inscribed sarcophagus lid originally from the village of Islâmlar and now in the Antalya Museum bears the name of a bishop and appears to be not earlier than the eleventh century. The inscription was read by Professor Mellink and converted into conventional spelling (the original being in twelve-syllable verse) by Professor Cyril Mango.[17]

+ Ὁ Κοιλαδηνὸς καὶ θεῖος θυηπόλος
   Ξεστὴς τῇ κλήσει καὶ ηρῶτος τῆς κοιλάδος
   πολλὰ βιώσας ἐν[θάδε . . .

16. Harrison 1979b, 237–38, fig. 12; 1986a, 73–74, pls. 2–3.
17. C. Mango, personal communication.

[The holy priest Koiladenos [either a family name or a term meaning, "native of the valley"], called Xestes, the first man of the valley,
having lived a long time [lies here . . .]]

Another sarcophagus, inscribed with crosses, was found at Sarılar, near
Choma, and has been dated to the eleventh or even the twelfth century.[18] It
had been recut and only the lid survives, but it may have been of classical
hog's-back type.

Gilevgi

Three forts overlook the Elmalı plateau. The first is the fortress of Gilevgi,
on the southern slopes of a freestanding hill, at the northern end of the
plateau. It was planned and photographed by Petersen and von Luschan in
the 1880s.[19] The walls are built of ashlar blocks, with rectangular towers.
These defenses are semicircular, and on the north and east sides the hill
drops sheer below the walls. It is a good strategic site, controlling the road
to the northeast, but there appears to be no definite evidence later than the
Roman period.

Armutlu

Some five kilometers south of the village of Akçay and nearly two hundred
meters above the plateau (near the village of Armutlu) is a strongly fortified
site overlooking the plain (fig. 74).[20] It lies on a spur of the Süsüz Dağ
(whose name means "waterless mountain") and is defined on the east side
by a defile, which carries a forestry road high through the juniper and cedar
forest to the Dokuz göl (lake) and then down again to Tekkeköy. The
ground slopes steeply to the north and drops away sheer to the south, so
that the south side needs no wall for much of its length. The plan of the fort
is approximately 250 meters square. It has one gate in the north wall and
two in the west, and the latter two open into a cemetery with some half a
dozen hog's-back sarcophagi. The masonry is massive, irregular, and without mortar. There are no towers. Inside are traces of buildings terraced into
the steep slope. Although it is not known when the fort was constructed, it
was certainly inhabited in the late Roman period, to judge from the abundant shards of local red fine ware. However, the ancient name of the site is
not known, nor is there any historical record for it.

18. Harrison 1984, 76.
19. Petersen and von Luschan 1889, 165, fig. 77, pl. XXIII.
20. Bean 1968, fig. 2.

Elmalı Dağ

The third site was the fort of Elmalı Dağ. The village of Bayındır lies some five kilometers northeast of Elmalı, on the lower slopes. From it a path leads westward up to the mountain through orchards and eventually through bare scanty pasture. For short stretches the path has the form of an old cobbled road, probably early Turkish. The road is some 1.5 meters wide, with a step every 2 or 3 meters. After two hours' walk along this path, it is possible to climb westward to one of the lower summits of Elmalı Dağ. There are magnificent views over both plains, from Gölova (Müğren) to Hacımusalar and below to Elmalı, seen from a height of around four hundred meters above the plain. Substantial walls of polygonal masonry and potsherds attest to a considerable settlement, although lack of time prevented a proper examination during my visit. A rock-cut boundary inscription at the summit of the ridge was seen in 1964 by Professor Mellink's jeep driver and a representative.[21] It gave the name of the site, to which the territory of Bayındır belonged, and this name was also recorded on a statue base from a small church near the village.

There are two late Roman towns in the mountains above the plateau. One is at Serkiz Alanı south of Söğle. The other is at Ovacık, which lies in the present *vilayet* (province) of Elmalı, but which may have been in the *territorium* of Termessos in Pisidia in antiquity.

Serkiz Alanı

The site of Serkiz Alanı is a two-hour walk from Söğle and is perhaps fifteen hundred meters higher than that village. It lies in a valley on the mountain of Bey Dağ, which is over three thousand meters above sea level. The summit of the mountain, marked by a cross, is said to be another four to six hours' walk away. There was more to be seen at Serkiz Alanı in the nineteenth century, when it was visited by Petersen and von Luschan,[22] than there was at the time of my visit, but at least there were Roman hog's-back sarcophagi, cisterns, three rock-cut tombs, and many limestone blocks. Serkiz Alanı has been thoroughly looted in the last two decades, and very few important stones are left now. I saw a pile of stones in Söğle, destined for limekilns in the same village, that had been brought down by tractor from the site (figs. 32–33). There were twelve working limekilns, which seemed to be an alarming threat to the remaining local sculpture. I was told that they were the only

---

21. M. J. Mellink, personal communication.
22. Petersen and von Luschan 1889, chap. 11.

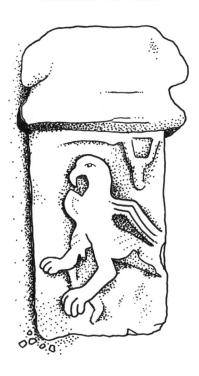

Fig. 32. Söğle; sculpture of eagle. (Drawing by Vicki Frenz from original photograph.)

kilns in Lycia and that they had been set up shortly before my visit in 1982. The stones included a characteristic ambo base above double steps and an Ionic capital with a cross, both pieces of about sixth-century date.[23] The ambo base is similar to the piece from Müğren described earlier in this chapter (fig. 79).

A traditional Lycian beehive, five meters high, was discovered near the road to Söğle (fig. 99). Its tall square structure was extraordinarily similar to that of the so-called Harpy Tomb of the early fifth century at Xanthos and to that of several other pillar tombs elsewhere in Lycia. The pillar is solid, and there is a wide cornice at the top, below the hive, to protect the honey from bears — and it may not be too fanciful to suggest that the same design would have protected the tombs from animals. A ladder gave access to the honey, which was stored in several hollow pine trunks. The bees lived there in the summer and were taken in winter to Ernes, which is a small village near the coast, about fifty kilometers away and a thousand meters nearer sea level. These traditional beehives are fast disappearing and are being replaced by a modern type of hive that can be transported

23. Harrison 1984, 76, figs. 6–7.

Fig. 33. Söğle; part of frieze with horses and riders. (Drawing by Vicki Frenz from original photograph.)

by truck. This seasonal movement follows the tradition of migration from the hills to the coast each autumn.

An interesting light is shed on the modern use of ancient monuments by the use of several antique cisterns in this area. These are used not for containing water but for storing goat cheese. In each cistern are eighty or so goatskins, each containing seventy kilograms of white cheese, which is sent down to Elmalı to the weekly market. Each kilogram used to sell for two or three dollars. The cisterns effectively contain the family fortunes.

The ways of the plateau seem to be very traditional, and examples of that tradition include a nineteenth-century timber granary, constructed using timber nails instead of iron (fig. 8 shows a similar structure in the Alakilise valley). There were similar buildings at Xanthos in the sixth and fifth centuries B.C. The town of Elmalı itself has several buildings of mud-brick construction. Still in use is a traditional cart, with solid wooden wheels (fig. 100). This type of cart has often been compared with illustrations on Lycian limestone tombs.[24]

Ovacık

Another interesting locality is the village of Ovacık, which lies about forty-five kilometers east of Elmalı. The modern track to the area rises to about

24. Mellink 1969, 290–99.

fifteen hundred meters before it drops down to a valley about eleven hundred meters above sea level, and the village is situated beneath the bare northern slopes of Bey Dağ, which itself rises to over three thousand meters. During my visit in 1980, my Turkish companions enjoyed cheerful hunting expeditions. They carried guns, in earnest pursuit of *keklik* (partridge) and *tavşan* (hares), which were abundant. For lunch, which we enjoyed in the restricted shade of one or two tiny trees, we had excellent partridge roasted over embers and wrapped in bread.

The region contains at least three ancient sites: a small Roman site near the modern village; a late Roman town in the valley to the south; and, between the two, to the north, a triangular fortification, of the same period or a little later than the town (figs. 34, 98).

At the northern end of the modern village lies at least one inscribed Roman sarcophagus. The village also yielded a fragmentary *Dioskouroi* relief, and its inhabitants showed us bronze coins ranging in date from the early Roman Empire to the time of Arcadius.

In a high secluded valley two kilometers to the south lie the remains of a small town.[25] These are rapidly disappearing as fields are extended and stones are robbed for building. The town was apparently unwalled and measured some three hundred meters across. There are the foundations of a number of fine buildings of dressed ashlar, including two churches, and the general impression is of a one-period settlement whose occupation was fairly short-lived. The cemetery is clearly visible outside the town (with five sarcophagi remaining) to the northwest, as are the surrounding field systems.

From this site, in 1975, were salvaged the remains of a large inscription, which the villagers had begun to break up for building stone to construct a new school, only a few days before my visit.[26] The lower part of a stele, inscribed on all four faces, was found almost intact, and about sixty meters away was discovered a scatter of recently trimmed fragments and chips, which appear to have constituted the upper section of the same block (see app. 2 and figs. 83–92).

The occupation of the site appears to have continued into the sixth or early seventh century. Limestone sculpture includes a twisting church capital and a cornice with a stylized grapevine which seems similar to cornices found at Arif and Alakilise (see chap. 2). There was also an enormous amount of late Roman local red pottery. In particular, there are so-called honey pots of late Roman local red glazed ware and small, well-made closed

---

25. Harrison 1979b, 235–37; 1980, 112–14, pl. XX.
26. Harrison 1979a, 530–31; 1979b, 237; 1980, 112, 114, pl. XVIIIa. See app. 2 below.

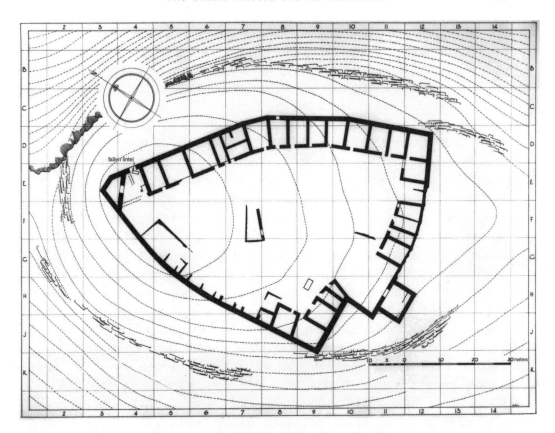

Fig. 34. Ovacık; plan of triangular site (*hisar*)

beakers with flat bases, strap handles, and clear rims. The pottery is from at least the fifth and sixth centuries in date and perhaps earlier.

There are also examples of this pottery from Islâmlar, Podalia, Choma, Tekkeköy, Yuva, Armutlu, Müğren, and Serkiz Alanı. However, there were none found at Söğle or at Gilevgi or Elmalı. There were some examples at Arif, at Dereağzı, and even at the Letöon near Xanthos. Many of the modern villages have also produced late Roman material, including pottery. Most of this pottery is local fine ware, and it would be excellent if a clear date and a general area could be established for it, to clarify the late Roman chronology.

A kilometer to the north, on a high hill with good views to the north and south, lies a triangular defended site, which was seen by von Luschan in 1882 and identified as a possible monastery (figs. 34, 98).[27] On two sides are steep slopes, but the south allows easier access and contains a gate, protected by a

___

27. Petersen and von Luschan 1889, 164; Harrison 1979b, 235, 237; 1980, 112–13, fig. 2.

tower. The interior consists of small rooms around a central area, where there were slight traces of a detached building. The masonry is irregular and without mortar. It seems to be late Roman or even slightly later, but it was not clear whether it was a refuge, a watch house, or even a monastery (although no church was found there).

Many sites of archaeological interest in central Lycia provide information concerning the period between the fourth and seventh centuries. However, there is little evidence of continuity of settlement during the Dark Ages, apart from that provided by the churches at Myra and at Dereağzı and by the site at Alakilise. No information about the activities of the population during this period has yet been derived from the study of sites on the Elmalı plateau, except for the evidence of the two sarcophagi of about the eleventh century (one giving the name of a bishop, the other with sculpture) described earlier in this chapter.

We do have some information on continuity of settlement in the Elmalı plateau area from the fourteenth century. There is the Selcuk mosque at Elmalı and the *türbe* (mausoleum) of Abdal Musa, a "wizard" at Tekkeköy, where they still have relics including his cloak, his wooden club, and various daggers. Furthermore, there is the practice of oily wrestling, which has taken place at Elmalı in August or early September annually since 1349. The town of Tekkeköy is said to have been founded at the same time, a hundred years before the siege of Constantinople in 1453.

Chapter 4

Phrygia and Amorium via
Antalya and Pisidia

The first three chapters of this book have illustrated that there is good archaeological evidence of continuity of settlement in Lycia during the sixth
and perhaps the early seventh centuries, as the study has moved from the
cities to the countryside inland. However, there is little or nothing concerning later periods. To obtain such information, excavation would be necessary to establish the chronology and the continuity of settlement in the area,
since there are few helpful texts, inscriptions, or even known roads.

In this chapter, the study will move into Pisidia and Phrygia, the real
center of Anatolia, in an attempt to find some settlement continuity. Research has been carried out on the coast, the hill slopes, the mountains, and
finally the plateaus, where at last there seems to be a most promising site
that may provide answers to some of the myriad questions concerning the
Dark Ages.

Ovacık, which was covered in chapter 3, was probably in the *territorium*
of Termessos in Pisidia in antiquity. The city of Termessos lies some twenty
miles northwest of Antalya. Its ruins, which are mainly of the Roman period, are built on and around a subsidiary peak of the Güllük Dağ, eleven
hundred meters above sea level. There are no known churches in the city,
but it has not yet been excavated, and Byzantine lists of bishoprics include
one of Termessos and Eudocia, which was located in the valley below at the
modern village called Evdir Han.

Jean Greenhalgh has written about Pisidia:

When we eliminate those traditional monuments of the Greco-Roman city
which might have fallen into disuse, after they have outlived their function — eg. pagan temples, theatres, agoras, and even bath-houses, gymna-
sia, stadia and council chambers — we are left with a handful of necessary
amenities, including the churches, the water-supplies, the streets, the

shops, and the workshops. If it is only those amenities of a city which were no longer essential, which fall into disrepair, one can argue only for urban transformation. An element of declining public pride and financial hardship might also be detected, but only when there is evidence for failure to maintain the necessary amenities, can one argue for urban decay, and, in some cases, for partial or total abandonment.[1]

Although this chapter is mainly about Pisidia and Phrygia, it will start at Antalya in Pamphylia, which is a port. Antalya has existed throughout the Hellenistic, Roman, medieval, and Turkish periods, although it may at times have had fewer than ten thousand inhabitants. The date of the church called Cumanı Camii in the town was probably late sixth or early seventh century.[2] It had rich Sassanian-type sculpture, which was reminiscent of the church of St. Polyeuktos in Constantinople in the early sixth century.[3] Antalya certainly represents an area of continuous settlement during the Dark Ages, as does Myra on the Lycian coast. Other similar sites can be seen at Sagalassos, Docimium, and Amorium and also at places along the banks of the Sangarius River, which runs northward to the Black Sea.

To the northwest of Antalya lay the city of Cremna, in Pisidia, which has been studied by Stephen Mitchell and Marc Waelkens.[4] This walled city is mainly Hellenistic to late Roman in date and is built on steep hillsides in an area between the modern towns of Antalya and Burdur. Cremna was known previously to have had three churches, including a basilica probably dating from the early Hadrianic period that was converted into a church, with relatively minor architectural changes, in the fourth century. Mitchell has found five new churches recently (which means there are eight in all on the site), and new surveys will doubtless reveal more. However, they are all of the late Roman period (having been built between the fourth and sixth centuries), after which the city of Cremna was probably abandoned.

The third site to be considered is Sagalassos. This site is again set high in the mountains, near Isparta, and existed from the Hellenistic to the late Roman period. Mitchell has carried out a survey, assisted by Waelkens, of an area about fifteen hundred meters above sea level.[5] This is high coun-

1. Greenhalgh 1987, 294 (paragraph shortened by permission).

2. Ballance 1955, 99–114, pls. 22–27; Aran 1970, 60–76, figs. 1–53; Grassi 1989, 83–104.

3. Harrison 1989b.

4. Mitchell et al., 1987–89. Editor's note: Professor Mitchell reports (personal communication to editor) that recent surveys have revealed many more fourth-/sixth-century churches in Pisidia than were known in the 1980s. He discusses evidence in "The Settlement of Pisidia in Late Antiquity and the Byzantine Period: Methodological Problems," in *Byzans al Raum,* ed. F. Hild (forthcoming).

5. S. Mitchell et al., 1987–.

try, and when Gertrude Bell went there in 1905, the theater of Sagalassos was covered with snow.[6] There are two churches, one of which is the so-called Transept Basilica. It is possibly fourth century in date, with a polygonal apse on the exterior, and the interior contains a frieze of masks and dancing satyrs. The arms of the transept can still be traced. There are indications that all the masonry was reused from a previous pagan building.

The so-called Ionic Basilica overlooks the lower agora and was built of material taken from the Temple of Apollo Clarius, which was probably erected in the second century A.D. The best preserved part of the basilica is the north arm of the transept. There is no evidence of mortar, which confirms that it was carefully constructed. Its date is thought to be in the fifth century.

Waelkens's survey produced an enormous amount of surface pottery. Much of it was fifth-century fine ware, and although it closely resembles that from Cyprus, it is probably local.

Moving to Phrygia, the Afyon Museum houses a collection rich in sculpture, which is not only Roman but also of later antiquity, including material from the tenth and eleventh centuries. It is one of the largest collections of Byzantine material in existence, and much of it is sculpted marble from the extensive quarries at Docimium, north of Afyon. However, material from the seventh to ninth centuries is still elusive.

Excavation at Sebaste (Selçikler), also in Phrygia, has revealed two groups of churches, one of sixth-century date and the other of about tenth-century date, which were excavated by Nezih Fıratlı.[7] The sixth-century church has a marble ambo of a form similar to those from Söğle and Müğren (fig. 79; see chap. 3).[8]

An excavation at the town of Aezani, southwest of Kütahya in west Phrygia,[9] had the investigation of the Roman baths as its main objective. However, another late Roman church was found, decorated with birds, a cross, and small sculptured heads and bodies. The marble is probably Docimian. The site is interesting, but again there is no evidence beyond the late Roman period.

The survey by Clive Foss at Kütahya established late Byzantine and Turkish occupation, but not late Roman.[10]

---

6. Catalog of the Gertrude Bell Archive, University of Newcastle upon Tyne, photographs F226–29.

7. Fıratlı 1979, 18–21.

8. For Söğle, see Harrison 1984, 76, fig. 6. For Müğren (ambo parapet now in Antalya Museum), see Harrison 1979b, 237–38, fig. 12; 1986a, 73–74, pls. 2–3.

9. Naumann 1979, 1980, 1982, 1984, 1987.

10. Foss 1985.

The Marble Trade

Docimian marble was much valued in antiquity and traveled by road, river, and sea to cities all over the Mediterranean, to Rome, to Lepcis, to Athens, and elsewhere. There was Docimian marble in the Temple of Mars Ultor in Rome, which was built by Augustus. Gigantic figures of the same material were brought to Rome by Trajan. The quarries are north of Afyon, near the present village of Isçehisar, and they have been developed extensively in the last twenty years. The marble travels by truck nowadays, but in antiquity it went by land and also by water, which was cheaper. It was the most expensive kind of marble, according to the Emperor Diocletian's Edict of Maximum Prices issued in A.D. 301.[11] It was also known as Synnadic marble, and the town of Synnada must have served as a distribution center, although the area was well inland and transport to the coast was expensive.

In the nineteenth century, William Ramsay wrote that the marble was only dispatched westward, from Docimium to Synnada (modern Şuhut), then to Apamea (Dinar), and eventually to the Maeander (Menderes) River.[12] Louis Robert agreed but considered that there were perhaps also routes to Izmir and Ephesus.[13]

Some Docimian marble went elsewhere, including Isauria, in the Roman period. For example, a gigantic Docimian sarcophagus weighing forty tons went to Sidamara in upland Isauria (the area to the south of modern Konya), presumably direct from the quarry. Similar sarcophagi traveled everywhere in Asia Minor—north, south, east, and west. In 1980, John Ward-Perkins published a distribution map (based on Ferrari, 1966), which was updated by Hazel Dodge and Bryan Ward-Perkins in 1992.[14] In 1982, Marc Waelkens published a book on the subject of Docimian Roman sarcophagi.[15] Now there is evidence for the use of Docimian marble in the Byzantine period.

A route from Docimium presumably ran eastward through the valley to Polybotos and then north to the area of Amorium. The terrain is fairly flat from the quarries to the head of the valley and then drops down to the plateau.

On this plateau is the site of Amorium, a town mentioned by Strabo. Before my survey and excavation of the site, finds from the area had included a Phrygian white marble tympanum (depicting an eagle) and other

---

11. Lauffer 1971.
12. Ramsay 1882, 290.
13. Robert 1962, 26.
14. Ward-Perkins 1980, 29, fig. 1; Dodge and Ward-Perkins 1992, fig. 52.
15. Waelkens 1982.

marble pieces, including capitals.[16] Similar capitals were found nearby at the villages of Emirdağ and Eskişehir.[17]

The source of the river Sakarya (ancient Sangarius) is near Amorium. It is not navigable above Gordium (near modern Polatlı) now, but it must have been a more substantial river in antiquity, before deforestation. However, it seems likely that the marble was transported by land across the plateau to the most convenient loading place, to be shipped down the river by barge or raft. The Sakarya becomes a major stream for one hundred kilometers as far as the Sapanca göl (lake) near Adapazarı. Thence it flows for another fifty kilometers to the Black Sea. If we assume that the marble had to travel on by land to Nicomedia (Izmit), this could have been the reason for the celebrated canal, proposed by the Roman writer Pliny the Younger to Emperor Trajan,[18] which would have linked Nicomedia with the Sapanca göl. The freight would have included Adapazarı, Bilecık (southeast of Nicomedia), and Docimian marbles. None of the routes were easy, as even the Maeander has narrow upper reaches and gorges.

The excavation of the sixth-century church of St. Polyeuktos in Istanbul[19] produced about forty-five thousand pieces of marble, mainly Proconnesian, but including about two thousand fragments of Docimian. It was probably new material, but even if it were secondhand, the question still exists as to whether it traveled west or north from Docimium.

Amorium

As previously mentioned, Amorium lies to the north of Docimium, about forty kilometers away. The ancient city is mentioned by Strabo the geographer, who lived from 63 B.C. until A.D. 19.[20] The name of Amorium was included on an inscription (see later in this chapter), which has been published in *Monumenta Asiae Minoris Antiqua*.[21] There are also Hellenistic and Roman so-called Greek coins minted in Amorium,[22] for example, a coin of Julia Domna depicting a temple containing a statue of Tyche (Fortune), who holds a cornucopia and a rudder. The temple is shown with four spirally fluted columns with Ionic capitals and a pediment.

Amorium lay at the eastern edge of the Roman province of Asia, on the

16. Harrison 1988, 182, pl. XXIVa–b.
17. *MAMA* 1 (1900): 230 (item 433); Eskişehir Museum, brought from Çifteler.
18. Pliny *Epistulae* 10.41.
19. Harrison 1986b.
20. Strabo *Geography* 12.8.13.
21. Harrison 1988, 180–81, pl. XXIIb.
22. C. J. Howgego in Harrison 1990, 216.

border of Galatia,[23] but in the late fourth century it was transferred to the new province of Galatia Salutaris. At first it was junior to the city of Pessinus, but it later became autocephalous (i.e., independent) and then metropolitan (a provincial capital).[24]

Information about Amorium's history appears in interesting Byzantine and Arab texts,[25] and even a short Byzantine epic, 201 lines long, written in the fifteenth century.

The town walls were reconstructed by the Byzantine emperor Zeno (474–91), according to Cedrenus, and an Arab text refers to a high wall, forty-four towers, and a wide moat. The town expanded in the sixth century into a civic and strategic center, and there is a late-sixth-century description several pages long by St. Theodore of Sykeon, who visited Amorium while traveling to Pisidia via the Sangarius River. In the seventh and eighth centuries, Amorium was the headquarters of the Anatolic Theme (military district), and it seems that whereas the First City (of the Byzantine Empire) was of course Constantinople and the Second City was Thessalonika (both in Europe), the Third City was probably Amorium.[26] There were other towns, such as Ephesus, Nicaea (Iznik), and Ancyra (Ankara), but these seem to have been comparatively small. The Arabic chronicler Tabari described Amorium as "the eye and foundation of Christianity, and more valued by the Greeks than Constantinople." It lay on a main route from Byzantium to Syria, and there were other good roads from Amorium to Ancyra and Iconium (Konya).

There were repeated Arab attacks on the city between the seventh and tenth centuries. A contemporary Arab text describes the attack, siege, and destruction of Amorium by al-Mutasim the Caliph in 838. He left Samarra in April with his army, carrying banners inscribed with the name of Amorium. The invading forces, in three separate armies, moved on Ancyra, which was captured in July. They then moved southwestward to Amorium. The writer mentions the high walls of the city, the defensive fosse, and the enemy's tents and wooden siege towers (each manned by between four and twelve men). Before the attack, al-Mutasim gave each man a sheep, ordering each to eat the best bits and to throw the rest into the fosse to fill it in. From the 1st of August the town was encircled, and attacks were directed against a known weak point, revealed by treachery. Although the Arab chieftains fought in the mornings and then repaired to their tents for lunch, the city was taken on the 12th and 13th of August.

---

23. Magie 1950, map facing p. 1616.
24. Ramsay 1890, 221–41; Darrouzès 1981.
25. Harrison 1988, 175–76 and notes; 1989a, 167–69 and notes.
26. Treadgold 1988, 41.

Part of the population sought refuge in a large church, where they were burned to death. The city walls were razed to the ground, and the place was left desolate. It was said that thirty thousand townspeople were either killed or captured. A sequel was the celebrated story of the Forty-Two Martyrs of Amorium, who were taken to Samarra but refused to embrace Islam and were executed there on 6 March 845. Tradition suggested that the city was then quite deserted. However, it seems to have been restored at some stage, because it was again destroyed by the Arabs in 931. When study of the site began, in 1987, it was believed that Amorium had become a simple village by the tenth century. However, the possibility that it still had the status of a town well into Selcuk times in the fourteenth century was soon under consideration, because of archaeological evidence. The area was deserted in the Turkish period, but in 1892 a small village of mud-brick houses was set up. It now consists of only about twenty mud-brick buildings (fig. 35) and a stone-built mosque and school (which closed in 1991). Its recent decline is linked particularly with the attractions of the nearby town of Emirdağ.

The site of Amorium lies in a wide plateau, near the headwaters of the river Sangarius in eastern Phrygia, 170 kilometers southwest of Ankara. The nearest modern town is Emirdağ, twelve kilometers away. All the neighboring villages are compartively affluent, except for the village of Hisarköy, which is built on the site of Amorium and is very poor. The area is about nine hundred meters above sea level, and the surrounding mountains are about two thousand meters high.

Amorium lies on the north-facing lower slopes of the mountains of Emirdağ, on a peninsula formed by two streams that conjoin (figs. 80–81). The plentiful springs and brooks flow northeastward to the river Sakarya (Sangarius), and there is good grassland to the north, wheat fields to the west and east, and rocky mountains to the south. Of the three Arab besieging armies in 838, the first set up its campsite two miles to the north, where there was good grass for horses. Were the springs and grasslands of that time similar to those of today? In addition, the streams or fosses are dry in summer. Were they similarly dry in the past, or was there water? There are modern wells and also some ancient ones in the village. No Roman aqueduct to the south has been found as yet, although local hearsay evidence indicated that it could have existed.

The Turkish authorities at Ankara issued a survey and excavation permit for Amorium in 1987 and in following years, and a survey of the site was carried out in 1987 (fig. 36).[27] Excavations began in August 1988, with a team of about a dozen archaeologists, assisted by the villagers, working for

27. Harrison 1988.

Fig. 35. Amorium; derelict farm buildings, Hisarköy. (Drawing by
M. A. V. Gill.)

about one month every year. The local harvest takes place in July, releasing
a large body of manpower, enhanced by the villagers' families (working in
Eskişehir, Afyon, and further afield) who come home at this time of year for
a "vacation." The declining local population has meant that it is easier to
find accommodation for the team, but an official excavation house and a
permanent storage depot were established in 1991 (fig. 37).

During the survey of the site, which is oval, a preliminary general plan
covering an area of about a kilometer and a half by nearly a kilometer was
drawn up. The plan includes the Upper Town (the "acropolis," or *hüyük*),
the Lower Town, and the city walls and towers. It also shows the two
streams or fosses that conjoin, a sewer, the necropolis, and quarries.

Upper Town

The hüyük, which is an artificial mound or tell, is three hundred meters long
by twenty-two meters or more high. It was probably continuously occupied
from the prehistoric period down through the historic and classical periods.

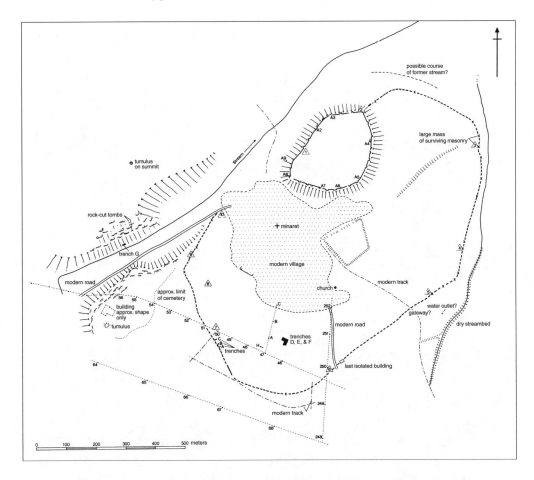

Fig. 36. Amorium; general survey (1987). (Drawing by H. G. Welfare.)

The Hittites named it Aura in the thirteenth century B.C.,[28] and the Romans and Byzantines used it as their Upper Town. Amorium was possibly restricted to this Upper Town in the Dark Ages, before the well-recorded siege of 838, and the account of the population of thirty thousand and the forty-four wall towers may be viewed with skepticism. There was a small late fort of irregular plan measuring about fifty by thirty meters in the southwest corner.[29]

In 1836 William Hamilton made a drawing of a late Roman gate in the Upper Town, but it has now disappeared. He wrote, "We reached the deserted and dreary site of what was once a populous city, and seldom have I

28. Garstang and Gurney 1959, 91, 94, 100.
29. Harrison 1991, 219.

Fig. 37. Amorium; dig house at Hisarköy. (Drawing by M. A. V. Gill.)

witnessed such a striking scene of solitude and desolation."[30] But he was only there for one day.

In the area of the Upper Town, a survey was carried out covering five hectares, which were subdivided into twenty-five-meter squares for recording purposes.[31] Methodical examination of the ground surface yielded coarse pottery, glass, lamps, marble veneer, metal objects, chert blades, millstones, ceramic counters and stoppers, and light industrial debris. On average, each full square produced about one hundred artifacts, as much, for example, as a similar exercise carried out at the city of Pessinus to the northeast of Amorium. Dating of the artifacts suggested activity on the site in the prehistoric, Phrygian/Hellenistic, Roman, Byzantine, Selcuk, Ottoman, and Turkish periods, with the principal periods being the Byzantine, Selcuk, and later.

The walls of the Upper Town were planned out by electronic distance measurement,[32] and the towers and three gates were identified. The walls consisted of large ashlar blocks, including reused Roman sculpture and architectural members, and presumably belonged to the period of Zeno

30. Hamilton 1842, 449.
31. J. A. Lloyd in Harrison 1990, 206–9.
32. H. G. Welfare in Harrison 1988, 176–80, 183–84.

(474–91). Work on the eastern section of the city wall revealed at least three clear phases, from the Roman period, the late Roman period, and a later period (possibly Selcuk). Structures included a Roman street, two houses with a yard and a street on a slightly different alignment to the previous one, and a house to the south that was cut by a rectangular tower and the perimeter wall.[33]

There is one large church in the northern area, which is probably late fifth or early sixth century in date. The apse, which contains Phrygian marble, is polygonal externally and eight meters wide internally. The church was about forty meters long and perhaps had four aisles. Green and blue glass mosaic tesserae were found in the narthex or atrium.[34]

There are some indications of a Selcuk settlement with a mosque in the fourteenth century, and a series of crude and impermanent structures was erected among the ruins of various earlier buildings. The northern room of the building inside the Upper Town gate provided a carbon-14 date of A.D. 1310–50.[35]

Lower Town

The Lower Town walls in the southwest are built of ashlar and rubble. There is a modern track to the south, which may have been a dry fosse, rather like that in the defenses at Constantinople.

Various excavation trenches were opened on the lower town walls.[36] One of them established that the wall was three meters broad, and a rectangular tower, incorporating several periods of construction, was found. There was another, triangular, tower, which was apparently contemporary and was well constructed of large ashlar blocks. Parallel examples for this triangular tower were found in Serdica (Bulgaria), Thessalonika (where they seem to be fourth century in date), and Xanthos (see chap. 1).[37] The late Roman dating accords with the text giving a date in the late fifth century, the time of Zeno.

In the triangular tower was found an Ummayad bronze weight of 535 grams (over one pound), dated somewhere in the period A.D. 690–750.[38] It

33. A. Claridge in Harrison 1990, 208–9, pl. XXXII; A. Claridge and I. Y. Sjöström in Harrison 1991, 218–20, pl. XLIIIa.

34. Harrison 1988, 180.

35. Harrison 1990, 209; A. Claridge and I. Y. Sjöström in Harrison 1991, 219–20.

36. N. Christie in Harrison 1990, 211–13, pl. XXXIIIb; N. Christie and I. Y. Sjöström in Harrison 1991, 220–22, fig. 4, pl. XLIIIb; N. Christie in Harrison et al. 1993, 150–51, pl. XXVII.

37. For Serdica, see Bobčev 1961, 103–45; for Thessalonika, see Spieser 1984, 74–75; for Xanthos, see Metzger 1963, 1, pl. 7.

38. Harrison 1989a, 173–74, pl. XLVIIIb.

is inscribed with a name of an Amir, who may have left it behind after one of the Arab sieges.

The one clear building in the Lower Town is a church.[39] The original structure is a basilica about thirty-five by twenty meters in size, which is certainly Justinianic (A.D. 527–65) or a bit later. It seems to have been an ornate building with rich marble cladding on the walls, shaped marble flooring, and mosaic-encrusted vaulting. But there were structural changes in a secondary phase, and later the plan changed from a basilica to a building with a central dome supported by four internal piers.

Analysis of the furnishings indicates that the church functioned at least into the mid–eleventh century, with signs of a revival of its role in the late tenth. Squatter and storage activities appear to have allowed for the basic survival of the building, with rough walling inserted between the piers to divide the space into individual rooms or stalls. These alterations caused the destruction of the decorative marble and painted plaster. In addition, two almost circular silos were built, one in the north aisle and one in the nave, of which one was skillfully lined with reused large voussoirs from the earlier building.

Finds from the church included two Docimian white marble capitals (now in the Afyon Museum),[40] other local marble pieces in several colors, a late Roman marble column plinth with an eleven-line inscription naming a saint and martyr (Konon),[41] and a piece of Byzantine marble templon architrave with decorative panels and a dedicatory inscription recording the restoration of the church (about tenth century),[42] perhaps when it was reconstructed with pillars and a dome.

There were certainly two other churches in the Lower Town.

Another important structure identified by excavation was a large late Roman building in the southern part of the town,[43] which seemed to be a palace or other official edifice, although it may never have been completed. It was constructed in concrete and mortar, but there was no evidence of a proper floor. The edges of the building were identified to the north, west, and south, but the east side could only be established by sondages, because it extended into a cultivated field. The west side of the building was lower, with a terrace.

39. D. A. Welsby and H. Dodge in Harrison 1991, 222–24, fig. 5, pl. XLIV; D. A. Welsby and I. Y. Sjöström in Harrison 1992, 207–11, pl. XLVII; I. Y. Sjöström in Harrison, et al. 1993, 149–50, pl. XXVIb.
40. Harrison 1988, 182, pl. XXIVb.
41. M. H. Ballance in Harrison 1992, 211, pl. XLVIIIa.
42. C. A. Mango in Harrison 1992, 212, pl. XLVIIIb–c.
43. Harrison 1989a, 171–73, pl. XLVI; D. Welsby and H. Dodge in Harrison 1990, 209–11, pl. XXXIIIa.

There was, however, a later level in at least part of it, with two firm dates from coins of the eleventh century (1082 and 1087). One of the trenches revealed two architraves and a capital, all of limestone, from the upper level. The capital was inscribed with an *M* and a small *k* and is about sixth century in date. The later levels included one copper Selcuk coin of the thirteenth century.

Inscriptions

There were twenty-three doorstones (tombstones) of familiar Romano-Phrygian type, dating down to the third century A.D., of which eight were never inscribed or lost their inscriptions when cut down for reuse in the Upper Town walls (fig. 82).[44] Six doorstones include fish, either singly or in pairs, in their decoration, and Sir William Calder suggested that this may have been a tactful way of saying that the deceased were Christians.[45] Other possible indications of early Christianity are the "hot cross bun" (a circle divided into four by horizontal and vertical lines) and the bunch of grapes, which might together symbolize the Eucharist.

Among the Roman inscriptions is a Latin tombstone inscription that is probably Trajanic (A.D. 98–117) or earlier.[46] Much of it is missing, but the translation is as follows:

> To the Spirits of the Departed and of Bellicius. Isochrysus, agent of Amorium of the associates of public concern of the 2.5 percent dues of the harbors of Asia, made this.

It refers to a *statio* (literally, harbor), a term that usually belongs to a sea-port, like Ephesus. This is the only inscriptional text of the name of Amorium so far known, apart from the Hellenistic and Roman (so-called Greek) coins.

Pottery

Study of the pottery has commenced,[47] but it will take some time to make sense of it. There are forty-three fabric types so far, including three local

44. M. H. Ballance in Harrison et al. 1993, 155–56; illustration in Harrison 1989a, pl. XLIV.
45. *MAMA* vii, no. 297 (cf. p. xxxix).
46. Harrison 1988, 180–81, pl. XXIIb.
47. L. Bown in Harrison 1990, 213–15; 1991, 224–28; 1992, 212–16; Bown in Harrison et al. 1993, 154; R. Tomber (fine wares) in Harrison 1992, 216, figs. 4–5; Tomber in Harrison et al. 1993, 154–55.

types, which form the vast majority. The finds include fine Roman wares of the fifth century, similar to those found at Pessinus or perhaps earlier. These Roman wares are local and not from west Asia Minor or Cyprus.

Small Finds

The miscellany of small finds includes several interesting groups of objects as well as individual items.[48] Glass is represented by a considerable number of window fragments, vessels, and bracelets, many of which have enameled decoration. Most of the small finds are domestic in character, but the ironwork includes arrowheads, although it consists mainly of nails of various shapes and sizes. Surprisingly few items of bronze have appeared, apart from a small human mask (which may have been attached to a piece of furniture) and part of an inscribed cross. The cross motif also appears on the handles of terra-cotta lamps. A group of undecorated lamps, each of open circular shape, appears to be of local design and manufacture. There are two earthenware stamps (one possibly for stamping bread) and four fragments from the statuette of a horse with harness and saddlecloth. A tile incised with concentric squares and cross lines may have been a gaming board.

Environmental Research

Some idea of the diet of the people of Amorium was gained from systematic sampling of environmental material.[49] Grains of wheat and barley, which are still cultivated today, were found. There was little evidence of legumes, and few pulses are currently grown by villagers. Grape pips were in evidence, and grapes may have been used to make wine or food. At the present time, there are a few vineyards near Amorium, and the grapes are used as dried fruit (*pestil*) or in an unfermented drink (*sira*). Animal bones were mainly sheep, goat, cow, horse, and, to a lesser extent, pig. Chicken bones were also present.

The excavation program at Amorium throws some light at last on the late Roman period and the Dark Ages. Most of the archaeological work on Roman and Byzantine sites in this part of Turkey has been done on the coast and in the southern mountains. Little work has been done in the central

---

48. Harrison 1989a, 173–74, pls. XLVIIb–XLVIII; M. A. V. Gill in Harrison 1990, 215; 1991, 228; 1992, 216–21; Gill in Harrison et al. 1993, 160–61, figs. 2–4.
    49. J. Giorgi in Harrison et al. 1993, 151–53.

area, except at the city of Pessinus.[50] It is therefore desirable that work on Amorium and its surrounding country districts (or *territorium*) will continue for many years. If there were another Roman and Byzantine site inland, it would be enormously useful for the purposes of comparison.

Amorium forms a good comparison with Constantinople, for it was clearly an important inland town during the Dark Ages. Roman Amorium lay on the edge of Asia, and it was later the main bulwark against the Arabs, protecting Constantinople, which by now had replaced Ephesus as the most important port.

This study began on the coast of Lycia and then moved through the mountains and the plateau of Elmalı to Pisidia, Phrygia, and Galatia. Finally, it came north to the plateau of east Phrygia. I myself began work thirty years ago in Lycia and then had a spell of six years in Istanbul excavating the large church of St. Polyeuktos, after which I returned to Lycia and finally went to Amorium. I have thus studied three samples of late Roman and Byzantine material, from Constantinople, Lycia, and Amorium—from the capital, mountain villages, and a city on the plateau. I hope to be able to link them somehow.

There is need for further excavation, to sort out the pottery into general periods and to establish some detailed pegs. Although digging in Lycia was considered, there are considerable disadvantages as well as advantages in excavating for material relating to the Dark Ages in such a coastal province. Central Anatolia, which is far from the sea, seemed a better proposition. Amorium has produced many coins, inscriptions, marble remains, local pottery, and other small finds. There are also many relevant texts of the later Roman period and some of a later date. The main problem, however, is the lack of comparison with other similar sites.

---

50. Lambrechts 1970–73.

Fig. 39. Dereağzı: church and south octagon, from southwest

Fig. 38. Dereağzı; church, from south

Fig. 40. Muskar; church, cornice

Fig. 41. Muskar; church, detail of cornice

Fig. 42. Muskar; church, fragmentary entablature

Fig. 43. Muskar; church, capital

Fig. 44. Capital of unknown provenance, Antalya Museum. (Photograph by James Morganstern.)

Fig. 45. Road from Alakilise to Muskar

Fig. 47. Alakilise; church complex of the archangel Gabriel

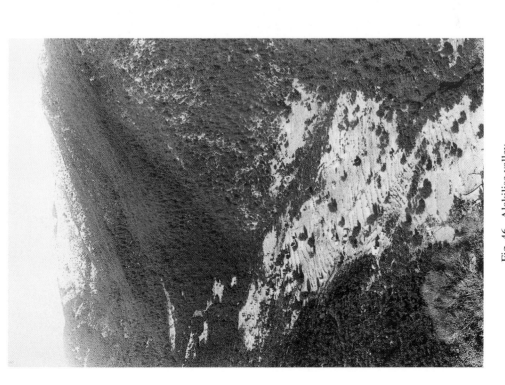

Fig. 46. Alakilise valley

Fig. 48. Alakilise; church complex of the archangel Gabriel, inscription recording restoration

Fig. 49. Alakilise; church complex of the archangel Gabriel, narthex entablature

Fig. 50. Alakilise valley; house in site A complex

Fig. 51. Alakilise valley; house C1

Fig. 52. Alakilise valley; entrance to rock-cut chapel at Saraylı

Fig. 53. View from Dikmen

Fig. 54. Dikmen; south apse of *triconchos* church, inner face

Fig. 55. Dikmen; apse of *triconchos* church

Fig. 56. Turant Dağ; north wall of baptistery of church complex

Fig. 57. Karabel; view of Sion monastery from northeast,
with monastery in foreground; Alacahisar lies beyond

Fig. 59. Karabel; Sion monastery, interior of east apse

Fig. 58. Karabel; Sion monastery, general view of *triconchos* church from southeast

Fig. 60. Karabel; Sion monastery, domed chapel: northwest corner
with pendentive and doorway from south aisle

Fig. 61. Karabel; Sion monastery, east wall of domed chapel

Fig. 62. Karabel; fortification wall of acropolis

Fig. 63. Devekuyusu; apse stonework of church

Fig. 64. Alacahisar; view of church from northwest

Fig. 65. Alacahisar; church, decorated voussoir

Fig. 66. Alacahisar; church, decorated spandrel

Fig. 67. View across Arycandus valley from the south

Fig. 68. Arif; main east gate of town

Fig. 69. Arif; northeast angle towers of town wall, from southeast

Fig. 70. Arif; town wall (southern sector)

Fig. 71. Arif; secondary street of town

Fig. 72. Arif; arched doorway in town wall, leading to tower 7 (west side)

Fig. 73. Elmalı plain; view of drained Avlan Lake

Fig. 74. Elmalı plain; view from Armutlu

Fig. 75. Elmalı; old minaret with stork's nest

Fig. 76. Choma; view from south

Fig. 77. Tekke; capital

Fig. 78. Müğren; capital

Fig. 79. Elmalı region; ambo parapet

Fig. 80. Amorium; aerial view

Fig. 81. Amorium; view from *hüyük*, looking northeast

Fig. 82. Amorium; Romano-Phrygian stele

Fig. 83. Ovacık; inscription I, side A.i, lines 1–10

Fig. 84. Ovacık; inscription I, side A.i, lines 11–22

Fig. 85. Ovacık; inscription I, side B.i, lines 1–13

Fig. 86. Ovacık; inscription I, side B.i, lines 13–25

Fig. 87. Ovacık; inscription I, side D.i, lines 1–13

Fig. 88. Ovacık; inscription I, side D.i, lines 11–24

Fig. 89. Ovacık; inscription I, side A.ii

Fig. 90. Ovacık; inscription I, side B.ii

Fig. 91. Ovacık; inscription I, side C.ii

Fig. 92. Ovacık; inscription I, side D.ii

Fig. 93. Alacahisar; rock-cut church

Fig. 94. Myra (Demre); St. Nicholas festival, church of St. Nicholas

Fig. 95. Muskar; east end of church

Fig. 96. Muskar; capital

Fig. 97. Karabel; view over Sion monastery, toward mountains above Kasaba

Fig. 98. Ovacık; triangular site (*hisar*)

Fig. 99. Elmalı plain; traditional beehive

Fig. 100. Elmalı plain; traditional cart

Appendixes

Nicholas of Myra and Nicholas of Sion

Nicholas was bishop of Myra in Lycia in the early fourth century. After a slow start, his cult spread with extraordinary rapidity in the Middle Ages — in the Byzantine provinces (there were at least twenty-five churches dedicated to him in Constantinople alone), in Russia (where he was to become one of the principal patron saints and latterly gave his name to two czars), in Italy (particularly after 1087, when his relics were transferred from Myra to Bari), and in western Europe, Britain, and Scandinavia. In about 1090, a magnificent Norman church of S. Nicola was constructed at Bari to house his relics. In Germany the cult was favored by Theophano (the Byzantine princess who was wife to Otto II), and from Bari it quickly passed to Normandy and to Lorraine. In England there are about 376 churches dedicated to St. Nicholas. This prodigious expansion seems surprising, as Nicholas did not suffer martyrdom, nor was he a soldier or a great healer. Nevertheless, he was one of the great miracle workers of the Eastern church and, after his translation to Bari in 1087, of the Roman church too. He was a popular saint — patron of the poor, schoolchildren, young brides, sailors, butchers, grain merchants, barrel makers, prisoners, and many others besides. He turns up in the most unlikely places, not only as Santa Claus in our department stores at Christmastime, but also in American purses — for the nickel was given its name in 1751 by the Swede Cronstedt, who named his newly discovered alloy after Nicholas, the presiding saint of copper mines.

In Eastern art, Nicholas is represented as a bishop, bareheaded, with a broad forehead, a beard, and usually a rather neat bone structure, although his features did not become standardized until the great expansion of the cult in the ninth century. In Western art, he was transformed into a Latin bishop, with miter and crosier, and from the fourteenth century he acquired special attributes: three purses of gold, or three boys emerging from barrels, or perhaps an anchor.

Tradition

Nicholas of Myra was born at Patara in Lycia, of rich and pious parents. It is said that on the very day of his birth, while he was being washed, Nicholas arose and stood straight up in his bath. Throughout his infancy, he rejected his mother's breast on Wednesdays and Fridays, which were fast days. He was, of course, a model schoolboy, and as he grew up, he sought how best to use his wealth. His good works, self-denial, and modesty led in due course to his elevation as bishop of Myra.

One story about Nicholas reports that one of his neighbors was reduced to poverty and saw no way out but to send his three daughters onto the streets. When Nicholas heard this, he was horrified. Wrapping up some gold in a cloth, he threw it in through his neighbor's window at night. In the morning, the father found the gold, thanked God, and prepared an honorable marriage for his eldest daughter; the same thing happened on a second night and again on a third. This is the origin of the gifts secretly delivered at night by Santa Claus (Sinterklaas in Holland).

A second story concerns a ship in difficulties in a storm. The sailors pray to Nicholas, who puts in a miraculous appearance to help them with ropes and tackle and still the storm. This story is overlaid with another, in which Nicholas succeeds in felling a demon-ridden tree sacred to Artemis. The demon, in fury, concocts an inflammatory oil and directs Artemis, in the guise of a nun, to present it to some sailors at sea. She then instructs them to rub the oil on to the walls of Nicholas's church. But Nicholas comes to the ship and exposes the fraud.

Another story involves a famine at Myra. Grain ships from Alexandria bound for Byzantium put into the harbor. (In fact, Myra was a regular stopping point for such ships, and there are the well-preserved remains of an imperial granary at its port of Andriake.) Nicholas went to the harbor and begged one hundred measures of corn from each ship. The captains refused, as the grain had been measured in Egypt and would again be measured in Byzantium. But Nicholas persisted, promising that the short measure would miraculously be made up. Nicholas took the grain, the famine was relieved, and at Byzantium the captains found, miraculously, that they had exactly as much grain as had been taken on board at Alexandria.

Finally, there is the story of the three boys who in a famine were butchered by an innkeeper. He pickled them in barrels and served them up as food. Nicholas, recognizing what he was being offered, was able to reconstitute the boys, limb by limb. This story, although it became famous, is a misunderstanding. The true story is of three officers who prayed to Nicholas after they were imprisoned by the Emperor Constantine and unjustly sentenced to death. Nicholas heard their prayer and appeared to Constantine in a dream, commanding their release, which came to pass. There were pictures of the three officers, the upper part of the body of each emerging from its prison tower. In its simplified form, the towers were taken to be barrels and the officers boys; thus a new legend was born, to become a part of the regular canon—and indeed part of an oratorio *(Saint Nicolas)* by Benjamin Britten.

I have described the legend[1] and the Western dimension of the cult. But what do we really know about St. Nicholas? Indeed, did he even exist? Or were there two Nicholases? The Vatican evidently had some doubts about him, as he was among various saints, like St. George and St. Christopher, who suffered official demotion in 1970. He is said to have been bishop of Myra under Constantine the Great, to have attended the first ecumenical council at Nicaea in 325,[2] and there to have punched the heretic Arius on the nose; but his name does not appear among the signatories to that council, and perhaps this story was apocryphal. Certainly most of the stories about him arose at a much later date.

The people now at Bari, where the bones of Nicholas are believed to lie, and in Apulia generally were extremely unhappy about his recent demotion, as Bari has little else of historical interest. The removal of the bones of Nicholas from Myra to Bari took place in 1087, just over nine hundred years ago. There has recently been a revival of interest in the saint, including a monthly magazine, the *Bollettino di San Nicola,* and visits to the church of St. Nicholas in Bari by Prince Charles and the Princess of Wales and even by the pope; and there are now close links between Bari and Myra. In 1983, a conference entitled the First International Saint Nicholas Symposium was organized at Myra and attended by the archbishop of Bari and the Orthodox metropolitan of Myra. A service was held in the church at Myra, which had lain unused for seventy years. This has now become an annual celebration.

One reason why the story of Nicholas is not quite so straightforward is because there were in fact two Nicholases, who by the ninth century were fused into one. The first was the fourth-century bishop of Myra already mentioned, and the second was the sixth-century abbot of Sion, in the territory of Myra.

An excellent vita of this abbot, St. Nicholas of Sion, who died in 564, was written by one of his colleagues.[3] The *Life of St. Nicholas of Sion* is a very

---

1. For a list of sources, see Ševčenko 1983, 25–27.
2. Ševčenko 1983, 18 n. 3.
3. Anrich 1913–17. Cf. Robert 1955, 197–208; Ševčenko and Ševčenko 1984.

valuable source and contains the names of thirty-five monasteries and villages that are to be sought on Alaca Dağ and that must have included Muskar and Alakilise (see chap. 2). At one time, the city of Myra, on the coast, was suffering from the plague, and the authorities accused Nicholas of Sion of preventing the farmers from bringing grain, flour, timber, and wine down to the city.[4] The archbishop sent two clerics to Sion, instructing them to arrest Nicholas and bring him back in chains, but Nicholas blamed the Devil for sowing slanders about him. The *Life* reports that his supporters asked him not to go to Myra, because there was "much wrath in the city on [his] account."[5]

The *Life* does not tell us whether Nicholas went to the city or not, but his next venture was to undertake campaign tours. Leaving the monastery well supplied with bread, wine, and gold, he would proceed to such-and-such a village, buy a number of bullocks, slaughter them, and invite everybody, young and old, to share the feast. Everybody fed, praised God, and praised Nicholas; and Nicholas, after a day's rest, then proceeded to the next village. There were ten such feasts on one trip in twenty days.[6]

We read in the *Life* about Nicholas's confrontation with a demon-ridden tree.

One day there came men from the village of Plakoma [near Myra], who fell down before holy Nicholas and said: "O servant of God, on our land there is a sacred tree in which dwells the spirit of an unclean idol, that destroys both men and fields." . . . Being so strongly urged, Nicholas, the servant of God, offered prayers, and came to the spot where the tree stood. Seeing the tree, holy Nicholas said: "Is this the sacred tree?" In response, the men . . . said to him: "Yes, Lord." And Nicholas the servant of God said: "What are those gashes in the tree?" They said to him: "Some man of old came to fell the tree with two hatchets, and an axe. And as he began to fell it, the unclean spirit snatched away the blades, and slaughtered the man, so that his grave was found at the roots of the tree." Offering prayers, the servant of God Nicholas—there being a crowd of nearly three hundred men, women and children to watch the workings of God, for none believed that such a tree, being sacred, was about to be felled—then the servant of God Nicholas knelt and prayed for two hours. And rising, he enjoined the men around saying: "In the name of our Lord Jesus Christ and of Holy Sion, come here, try and cut it down."

4. Ševčenko and Ševčenko 1984, 82–85.
5. Ibid., 84–85.
6. Ibid., 84–91.

A shiver ran through all those who were standing around holy Nicholas, and no one dared so much as to look at the tree. Then the servant of God Nicholas said: "Give me the blade and I will cut it down myself in the name of my Lord." Taking the blade, the servant of God Nicholas made the sign of the cross over it and struck the sacred tree seven times. The unclean spirit saw that the servant of God Nicholas had power from God, and when the tree was struck by Nicholas' holy hands, the unclean spirit cried out, saying: "Woe be unto me: I made for myself an ever-expanding dwelling in this cypress tree and have never been overcome by anyone; and now the servant of God Nicholas is putting me to flight, and no longer will I be seen in this place. For not only has he expelled me from my dwelling in the tree, but he is driving me from the confines of Lycia, with the help of holy Sion." . . . Forthwith, the tree swayed back by the will of God and moved toward the west, where it crashed. From that time on, the unclean spirit was no longer seen within those parts. And they all glorified God, saying: "One is God, who gave power to his servant against the unclean spirits."[7]

Nicholas of Sion also performed other miracles, including healings, exorcisms, summoning up of water, and the stilling of storms at sea. He traveled twice to Jerusalem—sailing from Myra and returning to Phoinix (Finike), Andriake (his intended landfall), or Tristomon (Üçağız)—and there were terrible storms on his travels.

And that night a great storm arose at sea, and the ship was about to be engulfed by the waves. When the sailors saw they were in jeopardy, they fell down before the servant of God, pleading and saying to him: "Lord Father, rise and pray for us, since we are in danger. For the wind and the waves are against us." And the servant of God Nicholas said: "The Lord hath a long arm, and will take care of his servants. Let us but have faith in Him, that if God wishes, He can save us." And bending his knee once again, the servant of God Nicholas prayed for long hours. And at the end of the prayer they all responded to him with the "Amen." And the wind and the waves stilled, and there was a great calm at sea.[8]

Nicholas worked in Lycia, mostly in the mountains above Myra, but also in Pinara, where he became bishop for three years.[9] It was a great distance

---

7. Ibid., 34–39.
8. Ibid., 54–55.
9. Ibid., 102–3.

from Sion to Pinara, beyond Xanthos, but for Nicholas it was just possibly far enough away from the archbishop of Myra, with whom he had not always had friendly relations.

The *Life of St. Nicholas of Sion* mentions a *martyrium* (witness church) of the fourth-century Nicholas in Myra[10] and a shrine to him at nearby Kastellon;[11] it also refers to an annual feast held in that bishop's honor.[12] Moreover, according to a sixth-century text called the *Praxis de Stratelatis,*[13] Nicholas of Myra intervened with the local authorities to rescue three innocent citizens of that town from unjust execution; later he appeared in person before the emperor Constantine in his palace bedchamber and ordered him to halt another execution, this time of three of Constantine's own generals who had been falsely accused of treason (the origin of the story of the three boys mentioned earlier). For the fourth-century St. Nicholas, therefore, there is only sixth-century evidence.

However, some new information seems to support the existence of the fourth-century bishop. This information concerns the name *Nicholas,* which certainly occurred in Greek, Hellenistic, and Roman times but was not common. The first volume of Peter Fraser's *Lexicon of Greek Personal Names* covers the Aegean Islands, including Euboea and Rhodes.[14] Of forty thousand entries, there are twenty-three instances of *Nicholas,* of which only three are Roman (early imperial) while the rest are from the fourth century B.C. and Hellenistic period. In the inscriptions of Lycia (*Tituli Asiae Minoris,* vol. II, nos. 1–3), including Xanthos, Patara, and Rhodiapolis, there are 1,230 inscriptions, including more than two thousand names, and there is mention of only one *Nicholas,* at Patara in the second century. Similarly, the inscription list of Termessus (*Tituli Asiae Minoris,* vol. III, no. 1), adjacent to Lycia, lists 944 inscriptions, which include about thirty-six hundred names, none of which is *Nicholas.* Furthermore, the majority of inscriptions in Lycia and, indeed, elsewhere are from the first, second, and early third century: there are very few from the late third, fourth, fifth, and sixth centuries. Although I have not checked in detail, I do get the impression that in Cilicia, Lykaonia, and Lydia, the name *Nicholas* was also rare.

Thus, Lycia and Termessus had very many inscriptions and only one mention of a *Nicholas* in the first three centuries. Of the fourth to sixth centuries, I have found about 130 personal names — from bishop lists, the *Life of*

---

10. Ibid., 28–29.
11. Ibid., 90–91.
12. Ibid., 108–9.
13. Anrich 1913–17, 1:67–91; cf. 2:368–75.
14. Fraser and Matthews 1987, vol. 1.

St. Nicholas of Sion, and inscriptions. There are sixteen instances of the name *Nicholas,* excluding the bishop of Myra. None was later than the time of Justinian. At least six of them were in the fifth century (one of whom was from the early fifth century), four were bishops, and one was the uncle of Nicholas of Sion.

Although in other provinces (e.g., Lydia and Cilicia), the name is still rare, it does look as if it was a more popular name in Lycia by the fifth century. This does not prove that there was a bishop called Nicholas in the fourth century, but it looks increasingly likely.

We thus have Nicholas of Sion, who is one hundred percent historical, and Nicholas of Myra, who is almost certainly historical. Development of the Nicholas tradition was slow. But certainly by the ninth century, these two figures, Nicholas of Myra and Nicholas of Sion, were merged by the literary tradition into one figure, and the miracles performed by Abbot Nicholas of Sion served to round up the rather bare life story of the original Nicholas, bishop of Myra.

Appendix 2

Three Inscriptions from Ovacık

Michael Ballance and Charlotte Roueché

The three inscriptions published here were copied by Martin Harrison at Ovacık in 1975 (inscription I) and 1978 (inscriptions II and III, on a single block). While Harrison reported their existence and cited some lines,[1] the extreme difficulty of reading inscription I delayed his publication of the group. Inscriptions II and III have since been seen and published; but we are publishing the three together here, because they are so clearly related to one another. We have worked from the squeezes, the notebooks, and the photographs, some of which are published here, but neither of us has seen the stones; we have no doubt that the readings can — and will — be improved by further study. The fragments that make up inscription I and the block that contains inscriptions II and III are under the care of the Antalya Museum, in their Archaeological Research Station at Elmalı.[2]

A wide range of study and excavation focused on Lycia and Pisidia has given a great deal more context to these texts than was available when they were first found. The lines from inscription I published by Harrison in 1979 have occasionally been referred to in subsequent publications; in 1996 Martin

We are very grateful to Elizabeth Harrison for the privilege of presenting the important material in these three inscriptions. We are greatly indebted to Nicholas Milner, Stephen Mitchell, Gary Reger, Christof Schuler, and Martin Zimmerman, who have all offered us extremely useful information, guidance, and advice on aspects of the texts, in the best spirit of the epigraphic *koinon;* the errors that remain are our own.

All the abbreviations are as in the *Oxford Classical Dictionary* (Oxford, 1996) with the following additions:

ACO   E. Schwartz, *Acta Conciliorum Oecumenicorum* (Berlin and Leipzig, 1922–)
BullÉp   J. and L. Robert, "Bulletin Épigrapique," annually from 1938 in *Revue des Études Grecques*
LBW   P. Le Bas and W. H. Waddington, *Inscriptions grecques et latines* (Paris, 1870)

1. See R. M. Harrison, "Nouvelles Découvertes Romaines Tardives et Paléobyzantines en Lycie," *CRAI* (1979), 237, whence the Greek text was published as *SEG* 29 (1979): 1514 and *BullÉp* 1980.488; more fully, "Upland Settlements in Early Mediaeval Lycia," *ACLA* 27 (1980): 112–14.

2. They were identified there by Prof. Machteld Mellink (Bryn Mawr College) and, in 1998, by Professor Gary Reger (Trinity College, Hartford), who transcribed II, III, and parts of I.

Zimmerman published an extremely useful article, reconsidering those lines in the light of the new publication of inscriptions II and III, and reaching conclusions very similar to those that we had also reached.[3] Stephen Mitchell has also discussed this material in a recent article.[4] An important study of the whole area by Christof Schuler came out just in time for us to consult it.[5]

Ovacık is reached from Elmalı; but it lies to the northeast, that is, in the direction of Termessos. There are three sites: a small Roman site; remains of a late Roman town; and, between them, a fortification on a hill.

The Texts

Ovacık I

Ovacık I is a long stele, inscribed on four sides: the stone was found in the late Roman town site in 1975. It is described in Harrison's notebook 1 (small fragments).

The lower part is a single block (see figs. 89–92). The upper block was found in fragments about sixty meters away and was taken to be from the same monument "although there is no join between the two halves" (notebook 1; subsequent study suggests that there is). The total height is approximately 2.90 meters. The two chief stones are apparently the upper and lower blocks of a large composite monument. Both are damaged and fragmented into several substantial pieces and some very small fragments. Harrison was able to restore the majority, but some fourteen very small fragments remain unassigned. Both upper and lower blocks are inscribed on all four sides and taper slightly. In our publication, we have lettered the faces (A–D).

The upper, smaller block (i) is made up of four large and sixteen smaller fragments. It measured some 1.31 meters in height. The faces broadened in width from top to bottom, from ca. 0.31 to ca. 0.42 meters. There is a rectangular dowel hole (0.02 × 0.02 × 0.02 m) in the center of the top face.

The lower, larger block (ii) was 1.565 meters in height. The width of the faces broadened from ca. 0.42 meters at the top to ca. 0.50 meters at the base.

The letters measure 0.025–0.03 meters; they are written between lines, which are ca. 0.04–0.05 meters apart. They were cut on faces that had not

3. M. Zimmerman, "Probus, Carus und die Räuber im Gebiet des pisidischen Termessos," *ZPE* 110 (1996): 265–77.

4. S. Mitchell, "Native Rebellion in the Pisidian Taurus," in *Organised Crime in Antiquity,* ed. K. Hopwood (London, 1979), 155–75.

5. Chr. Schuler, *Ländliche Siedlungen und Gemeinden im hellenistischen und römischen Kleinasien,* Vestigia 50 (Munich, 1998).

been well prepared for inscribing, so they vary considerably in shape and size; sigma is square, omega is angular, and alpha has a straight crossbar.

Ovacık I.A.i (figs. 83–84)

The text is made up of an upper and lower part, joining at line 11. There is an uninscribed area of ca. 0.15 meters before the text begins. In this is a dowel hole (0.035 × 0.017 × 0.03 m) at 0.08 meters from the top, set centrally, and below it is what may be a graffito of a sun.

Contents

This is the only side that clearly opens at the beginning of a document; it is therefore very probably the first side.

Lines 1–22 appear to be a letter from [M.] Aurelius Ursio, *dux,* to Hermaios, son of Askoureus.

Text

```
        [? Μ. Αὐ]ρ. Οὐρσίων ὁ δι-
        [ασή]μότατος δοὺξ
        ['Ερ]μαίῳ 'Ασκου[ρ]-
        [έως] v. χαιρεῖν. v.
    5   [ἅμ]α τῷ λαβεῖν
        [τ]αῦτα γράμματα
        τοὺ[ς] ν[ε]αν[ί]σκους
        [ἐπ]ιλέκτους δεῖ
        [πο]λείτας ΤΟΝΑ
   10   [ . . . ca. 7/9 . . . ]ΛΤΟΝ
        Ι[ . . . ca. 11/13 . . . ]Ι [ἡ]-
        μέρων Ι[ . . . ca. 7/9 . . . ]
        ΘΕ αὐτοῦ εἰς Κρη-
        μνα ἀγαγεῖν φρον-
   15   τίσον παυόντων
        παρ' ὑμῶν ἐκεῖ ΚΕ [?]
        μελλόντων ΚΑΘΕ-
        Ε[ . ]ΞΕ[ . ]ΔΩΡΗΝ οἷα ἐς-
        ται ὅτε [ . ] ΕΛΩΝ χρυ-
   20   σόν. . ]ΗΚΕΙΝ πα-
        ρασκ ΕΘΗΝΑΙ δῶ-
        ρον τείνας· ἔρρωσο.
        [ . . . ca. 12/14 . . . ]
```

Apparatus

Lines 1–9: These lines were on a fragment brought in by M. Mellink.
1–2: These lines were originally read by Harrison as τῶν φρουρείων ὁ διασημότατος δούξ; other scholars have cited this phrase from Harrison's preliminary publication.
Line 10: T might be E, P, I.
Line 12: M might be N, H.
Line 13: αὐτοῦ might be ἄρτου.
Line 16: Π might be T; final E might be T.
Line 17: Final E might be H.
Line 18: First E might be Π; Δ might be A.

Ovacık I.A.ii (lower part; fig. 89)

Contents

While the opening is not clear, from at least line 3 this is a list of acclamations in honor of Hermaios, requesting the prolongation of his office of "brigand chaser." The acclamations were perhaps to be sent to Hermocrates (line 3).

For a translation see below, p. 110.

The line breaks at lines 29–31 are not certain.

Text

```
   [ . ]εἰρηναρχ[- . . . ? Ἑρμοκρ]-
   άτει ἀγνῶς [ . . . 6/7 . . . ]
   [ . ]Ἑρμοκράτει· Ἑρμ[αῖος]
   [? v.] Ἀσκουρέως τῇ πόλε[ι]
 5 ἵνα δυνάμε θα ζῆσαι.
   ὁ ὑπὲρ τῆς πόλεως ἐπ-
   ιδημείτω. ὁ ὑπὲρ τῆς εἰ-
   ρήνης ἐπιδημείτω. το[ῦ]-
   το συμφέρει τῇ πόλε[ι].
10 ψήφισμα τῷ λῃστοδ[ει]-
   ώκτῃ. ὁ εὐγένης λῃ[ς]-
   τοδειώκτης τὴν π[ό]-
   λιν φρουρείτω. ὁ λῃσ-
   τὰς φονεύσας τὴν
15 πόλιν φρουρείτω.
   ὁ ἐκδεικήσας τὴν
```

πόλιν τὴν πόλιν *vac.*
φρουρείτω. ὁ πολάκι[c]
ἐκδεικήςας τὴν π[ό]-
20   λιν ἐπιδημείτω. ὁ ἀ[ν]-
νώνας ΕΝΝΕϹΑ[. .]
πέμψας ἐπιδημεί[τω].
ὁ ὑπὲρ τῆς [ε]ἰ̣ρ̣ή̣[ν]η[c]
ἐπιδημείτω. Ἑ[ρμαῖ]-
25   οc ἐπιδημείτ[ω. ? ὁ υἱ]-
ὸc Ἀσκουρέωc ἐ[πιδη]-
μείτω. Ἑρμαῖος Ἀ[σ]κ[ου]-
ρέωc ληcτοδει[ώκ]-
τηc ἕωc ζῶμεν. ἐπι[δη]-
30   μείτω ἵνα δυνάμεθα [ζῆ]-
σαι. κατὰ τὴν κέλευcιν τοῦ ἡ-
γουμέν[ο]υ ἐπιδημείτω. ὁ π[ο]-
λάκιc cῴcαc τὴν πόλιν ἐπιδη-
[με]ίτω. ὁ τροφὰc τῇ πόλει πέ[μ]-
35   ? *vac.* ψαc ἐπι-   ? *vac.*
? *vac.* δημείτω   ? *vac.*

Apparatus

Line 1: Harrison saw traces of a line above.
Line 2: ΑΤΕΙΛΕΝWϹ Harrison.

Ovacık I.B.i (figs. 85–86)
There is an uninscribed area of ca. 0.06 meters before the text begins. The face is worn, particularly at lines 18–22. The upper fragments join the lower at line 13.

Text

καὶ ἐξ ἑτέρων [. . . .]
τε ἔγνων ΜΑΛΙ[. . . .]
Μ̣Ι̣Νδειϲεται ΕΑΝ̣ [. . . .]
Τ̣ΗΤΑΙ ΕΠΙΞΑΤΗΙ[. . . .]-
5   νείαν τὴν οὖϲαν [. . . .]
κώμαιc ταῖc π[αρ᾽? ὑ]-
μῶν ΑΝΓWΕΧΘ[. . . .]
εἰc τὴν Τερμηc[έων]
πόλιν [ἵ]να τοῖc Ε[. . . .]

10 ṬAΓ [. . .]ṆOIС̣Ṇ[. . . .]
    [. . . . . .]φρουρα[. . . .]
    [. . . . .]ΑΝΕΝ̣[. . . .]
    ἀννῶνα παρεχ[- . . . .]
    λείπειν αὐτοῖς[. . . υ̇]
15 πὸ τῶν ἀρχόντ[ων . .]
    ΓṆWN καὶ Κ[.]ΗṂ[. . . .]
    ταῖς κώμαις ΕΥ[. . . .]
    Ṃ ΕΝΑΕ[?]С̣ΒΟ̣С̣ΤΑ̣[. . . .]
    [. . .]С̣Ε[. .]Ο̣ṂΠΟСΚ[. . . .]
20 ṆΟΙ̣Π̣ΑΙΑСΧ̣ΓW[. . . .]
    [.]ΠΑṬ [. .]ΑΜΠΕΖΑ̣[. . . .]
    [χ]ω̣ρίς τιṇ̣ος ὑπε[. . . .]
    του [.]Π [. .]С̣Α̣ṆṬΕ[. . . .]
    [. . . . . ἡγε]μόνες[. . . .]
25 [. . . . .]ΧΟΜΑΙ̣[. . . .]

Apparatus

Line 1: P could be B.
Line 3: M could be H; I could be Y; C could be Ξ; second N could be M.
Line 4: First T could be Γ, C; third T could be Y, Π.
Line 5: Schuler conjectures [ἐν ταῖς]
Line 7: NΓ could be MP. Schuler conjectures ἀνενεχθ[είσαις]
Lines 9–11: Schuler conjectures τοῖς ἐ[κεῖ τε]-/ταγ[μέ]νοι ςτ[ρατ/ιωται]
Line 10: T could be Γ.
Line 12: Final N could be KI.
Line 13: EX could be CY.
Lines 15–16: Schuler conjectures . . . ἔ]γνων
Line 16: M could be Π, W.
Line 18: M is very doubtful; first C could be K.
Line 19: First C could be E, Γ; Π could be T.
Line 20: N could be W; Π could be K; X could be K; Γ could be E, P.
Line 21: Z could be Ξ.
Line 22: N could be Δ.
Line 23: CAN could be ΑΛW.
Line 24: C could be P.
Line 25: I could be C.

Ovacık I.B.ii (fig. 90)
We have no text.

Ovacık I.C.ii (fig. 91)

The upper part (i) is lost, and it is not clear how long the full lines are in the lower part, which survives.

Contents

The people at line 3 may be the same people as in line 22 and inscription II, line 2. Line 17 ought to be the opening of a new document, the letter from [–]lios Aquilinos to Hermaios and the other *protokometai*. If so, line 23 is probably not a date.

Text

```
       [ . . .
       [ . . . . . .]ΔΟ[ . . . . . . . ]
       [ . . . . ]ἐποιης[- . . . . . ]
       ΑΜΛΔΕΨΝΤΨΝΗϹ [ . . . . ]
       [ . . . ]ἐφεδρεύοντι[ . . ]
   5   [ . ]τῃ πόλει κατηγε [ . . ]
       Ο τὴν κώμην ΔΗ[ . εἰ]-
       ρηναρχον μὲν ΠΡΟ[ . ]
       ΑΙϹ Μαρ. Αὐρ. ΗΛΛΨΑΦ[ . ]
       ρου ΒΟ[ . . ]ΑΔΟΥ καὶ βο-
  10   υλευτὴς καὶ ΔΗΖ[ . . -]
       αρχος Α [ . . . ] Μ [ . ]ΨΟΚ [ . . ]
       [ . ]αις ΙΛ [ . . ]ΑΤΕΙϹΛΗΙ
       [ . ]ϹΟΙ Ἡλιοδωρο[-. ] Ἑρμ-
       [έ]ου καὶ Ν [ . ]ΑΝΕΥ [ . ]ΙΕΜ
  15   [ . . ]ΝΟϹ καὶ ὑποφύλαξ [? τοῦ]
       [ε]ἰρηνάρχου σὺν ΕΥ[ . ]
       [ . . -]λιος Ἀκυλεῖνος
       διασημότατος ἡγ[ού]-
       [με]νος Ἑρμέῳ Ἀσκου-
  20   ρέως καὶ τοῖς λοιπ[οῖϲ]
       πρωτοκωμήτεϲ[? τῶν]
       ΑΛΛΝΕ[ . ]Ν χερεῖν·
       [ . ] ΝΕΤΕΙΑΚΤΤΑϹ
       [ . ]ΑΤΕ [ . . ]Κ [ . ]Η[ . . .
       [ . . . At least 4 lines follow.
```

Apparatus

> Line 3: It is tempting to see the name of the village here. M could be Π; Λ could be Δ, Λ; Δ could be M, Λ; T could be O; W could be Δ; C could be O.
>
> Line 5: Λ could be K, Y; T could be W, I; E could be Θ.
>
> Line 6: O could be Ξ; first N could be K; HN are in ligature.
>
> Line 8: Second P could be C; Φ could be O. Zimmerman suggests Ἡλιοδώ/ρου.
>
> Line 9: First B could be P.
>
> Line 12: Final I could be Γ, E, C.
>
> Line 13: P could be B; third O could be T.
>
> Line 14: E could be C.
>
> Line 15: O could be E.
>
> Line 16: Second N could be W; E could be B, Λ, Θ; Y could be I.
>
> Line 20: W could be H.
>
> Line 22: Again, the text appears to contain — and conceal — the name of the village.
>
> Line 23: First Λ could be Δ; K could be T; second T could be Y, Ψ.

Ovacık I.D.i (figs. 87–88)

The upper edge survives, showing that, as in A, there was a substantial empty space above (about 0.15 meters, so space for three to four lines). In this space, there seems to be the graffito of a small star.

The upper part is on a single block, broken at right, ending at line 10. The next section is on the same block as A.i.11ff.; it is therefore complete at the right side.

Text

```
        πόλιν κω[ . . . . . . . ]
        ΑC ἐπιδημε[ίτω . . . . . ]
        ΒΟΥΛΗ Ἑρμ[αῖος ? . . . ]
        [ . . ]ἀγορανο[μ- . . . . . . ]
    5   [ . . . . . . . ]Μ[ . . . . . . . ]
        [ . . . . ]ϹΑ[ . . . . . . . . . ]
        [ . . . . . . . . . . . . . . . . . . . ]
        [ . . . . . . . . . . . . . . . . . . . ]
        [ . . . . . . . . . . . . . . . . . . . ]
   10   [ . . . . . . . . . . .  . . . . . . ]
        [ . . . . . ἐ]πιδη[μείτω ? . . . . ]
```

[. . . . .]ΛΥΡΙΟ[. . . . . .]
[.]ΓΗ[. . .]ΕΜ[. . .]οὐδὲ
[. .]ΕΠΙΦ[. .]ΥΔΕΤΗ
15 [.]ΡΛΟΥΑ[.]ψηφιϲ
[.]ω Ἑρμα[ί]ω ΠΕΜ[.]
ΘΩΤΕ [.]ΗΧΙ̣ϹΕΙΑ[.
ΕΧΕΛ[.]Ẉ̣ΕΥ̣Ι̣Ẉ̣[. .
ΗϹ νεικηφόρων
20 παιδα[. .]ΕΙΚΗΛ
ΑΛ̣[.] ὑπὲρ τῆϲ πόλ̣[εωϲ
[. . . .]ΠΙ̣ϹΜΑΚΛΚ
ϹΟΙ[[. . . . .]ΔΟϹ [. . .
[. .]ΛϹΠΙ̣Υ̣[. . .

Apparatus

Line 1: ? πόλιν κώ[μαϲ τε πᾶϲ]/αϲ
Line 3: B could be K, X; H could be EI.
Line 4: First O could be Θ; second O could be K.
Line 12: P could be E.
Line 13: ΓΗ could be EN.
Line 14: Π could be B.
Line 17: W could be M.
Line 18: First W could be M.
Line 19: EI could be A.
Line 20: Second A could be W.

Ovacık I D.ii (fig. 92)
The block is in relatively good condition to the right, but the left side is largely lost.

Text

[. . . . . . .]Ι̣Ι[. . . . . .]
[. . . .]Ṇ καὶ ΤΑϹΚ̣Ε[. . .]
[.]ἔ̣δει ὥϲτε ἐν ἀϲφαλί-
[α̣ . .]ΔΗ μετὰ δὲ τὰ πά̣[ν]-
5 [τα ἀ̣]ϲφαλῶϲ ποιηϲα̣ι[. .]
[. . .]π̣άλιν π̣ρ̣οτρέπο-
[με]ν̣ ἀνήκειν εἰϲ τὴν
[λα]μπρὰν Τερμηϲέ-
[ων] πόλιν καὶ ταύτην

10   [. . .]ΤΕ χείϱισε μεταξὺ
    [. . . τῶ]ν π[ϱ]ωτευόντων
    [. . . .]ΝΑΝΑ καὶ τῶν βο[υ ?]-
    [λευτ]ῶν πολείτων καὶ
    [τῶν ν]εανίσκων φϱουϱ-
15   [. . . .]ΟΥΝ[. .]ΘΩΔΕΦΑ
    [. . . .]Η χεὶϱ στϱατιωτ [- .]
    [. . . .]Ε ἐφεστῆκε [.]
    [. . . .]ΓΗ ἥτισουν
    [. . . . .]μεϱιμνοΙ[.?]
20   [. . . . . .]ησει πεϱι
    [. . . . .]ταμιαΥ[.]
    [. . . . .]γαϱ [. .]
    [. . . . .]οἶκον
    [. . . . .]ΞΕΙΝ[.]
25   [. . . . .]ΠΑΡΕΞΙ
    [. . . . .]ΟΕΖΕΥΧΟ
    [. . . . .]ΑΝΤΙ vac.
    [. . . . ? vac.

Apparatus

Line 4: First Δ could be A; Schuler conjectures εἶν]αι.
Line 5: Final I could be C, N.
Line 9: THN are in ligature.
Line 10: First T could be K: perhaps με]τεχείϱισε
Line 12: First N could be KI; second N could be Λ.
Line 13: Second WN are in ligature; K could be T.
Line 24: Ξ could be C.
Line 27: Final I could be A.

Ovacık II and III

Ovacık II and III were copied by Harrison in 1978 (notebook 1, pp. 148–50) and again in 1980 (notebook 2, pp. 102–9). They were found again by B. Iplikçioğlu and A. and G. Çelgen and published by them in *Neue Inschriften aus NordLykien,* vol. 1 (Vienna, 1992), nos. 2 and 3, pls. 4, 5 and 8 (the latter are photographs of good squeezes); they were republished from that publication as *SEG* 41.1390 with emendations by H. Pleket. They were republished from these publications by Zimmerman in "Probus, Carus und die Räuber," 267–68; copied by Gary Reger in 1999. The two inscriptions are on panels (III on one measuring 0.89 × 0.37 m; II on one measuring 0.89 × 0.36 m) recessed on the face of a long block (2.29 m long × 0.52 m high × 0.60 m deep) now in the courtyard of the Elmalı museum. III is to the left of inscription II. The letters average 0.03 meters in size. In III.6 there are abbreviation marks: a bar over the initial M of Μαρ, and a vertical with dots above and below after ΑΥΡ.

For illustrations, see the publication of Iplikçioğlu, Çelgen, and Çelgen.

Ovacık II

Text

    Οὐαλ. Εὐήθιος ἔπαρχος *vac.* Κιλιορτῃ
    προοίκῳ κώμης ΛΛΛΛεων χαιρεῖν.
    ἐπειδὴ πυνθάνομαι ἐκ τοῦ cυcτήματ[οc]
    τῶν ἐπιπολαcάντων τῇ Τερμηcέων [χώ]-
5   ρᾳ λῃcτῶν ὑπολελῖφθαι [οὐδένα] περὶ
    τὴν ἀποικίαν καὶ πέπ[εισμαι ? . . .
    διὰ τοῦ cυνλημφθῆ[ναι . . .
    [. . .

Apparatus

Line 1: Εὐήβιοc Harrison; Εὐήθιοc Iplikçioğlu
Line 2: Harrison conjectures Ἀδαλέων; Pleket (*SEG*) cj. Α[σκουρ]εων, Zimmerman conjectures Α⟨σ⟩[κουρ]εων; Reger reads ΛΗΜΕΩΝ.
Line 4: Τητερμηcέων Iplikçioğlu, corrected by Zimmerman
Line 5: Ῥαληcτων Iplikçioğlu, corrected by Zimmerman; nothing after ΦΘΑΙ, Iplikçioğlu; Zimmerman conjectures [τινάc ὡc πάcχειν]
Line 6. καὶ ΠΕ[. . . Harrison.
Line 7. ΔΙΑ might be ΔΡΑ.

Ovacık III

Text

    βουλῆc *vac.* δήμου *vac.* δόγμα
    τὸν ἀξιολογώτατον καὶ ἐνδοξό-
    τατον καὶ εἰρήνηc προcτά[τη]ν ἀρχι-
    ερέα γενόμενον τοῦ ἀνεικήτου Cεβαcτοῦ

5 καὶ τῶν ἐπιφανεστάτων Καισάρων καὶ πᾶσαν λει-
   τουρ[γ]ίαν τελέcαc *(sic)* Μαρ. Αὐρ. Κιλιορτην υἱὸν τοῦ γε-
   [ν]ομένου Μαρ. Αὐρ. Ἑρμαίου Ἀcκουρέωc προcτάτου
   [τῆc εἰρην]ηc [? γεν]ομένο[υ]

Apparatus

   Line 1: δογματι Iplikçioğlu
   Line 3: ΤΑΤΗΝ Ip., ΤΑ[. .]Ν Harrison
   Line 5: ΛΕ Harrison, ΛΕΙ Iplikçioğlu
   Line 6: ΤΟΥΡΓΕΙΑΝ Iplikçioğlu
        ΚΙΛΙΟΡΤΗΝ Iplikçioğlu; at end, ΓΕ Iplikçioğlu
   Line 7: ΝΟΜΕΝΟΥΜΑΡ Iplikçioğlu
        ΑCΚΟΥΡΕW[C . . Iplikçioğlu
   Line 8: [12] . . . C[. . . . .]ΜΕΝΟ[. . . Iplikçioğlu.

Commentary

The Documents

Inscription I

The outline of the contents of the sides is as follows:

A.i.1–22: A letter from Aurelius Ursio, *perfectissimus dux.*
A.ii.(?)1–36: A series of acclamations for Hermaios, son of Askoureus.
   He is a brigand chaser and has protected the city: these lines request
   that he remain in office, probably as *eirenarch* (an office that has to be
   confirmed by the Roman authorities).
B: We only have the upper part. This starts in the middle of a text, and
   the *vacat* above it is shorter than that in A or D. It may well, therefore,
   follow C.
C: The upper part is missing. The lower part has a document with, perhaps, a list of local officials (?). Then, at line 17, a letter begins, from
   [–]lios Aquilinus, apparently a *perfectissimus dux,* to Hermaios and the
   other *protokometai* of the community.
D: This also starts in the middle of a document. There is not much to
   make out, but the first lines would fit well with acclamations: so D may
   continue A.

Inscriptions II and III

These are on two adjacent panels set into a long block that presumably formed part of a monument. Both honor Kiliortes, the son of Hermaios (son of Askoureus), who appears in inscription I: inscription II is a letter, apparently congratulating him on the suppression of brigands, while inscription III is a resolution in his honor by a council and people (so, by a city).

Date

Inscription I and inscriptions II and III refer to a father and a son, respectively. They cannot be more than twenty to thirty years apart in date, and they could be extremely close, since father and son could have been active at the same time; it is indeed more economical to assume that the men were active contemporaneously, particularly since they are both concerned with controlling brigands.

M. Christol published a list of third-century officials with the title of *perfectissimus dux,* used of Ursio in inscription I and first found at the end of the reign of Gallienus.[6] While Ursio's exact function is uncertain, Aquilinus, in the same document, is described as *perfectissimus hegoumenos,* which seems to mean that he was a governor. The earliest known equestrian governor in the area is Terentianus Marcianus, *perfectissimus dux,* now known to have been in office in 278.[7] The governor of Lycia was of *clarissimus* rank certainly by 363 and probably by the reign of Constantius II (337–61).[8]

Kiliortes (inscriptions II and III) was high priest of a single emperor and his sons. While such a position would probably still have been possible under Constantine, the office is more easily accommodated in the third century than in the fourth—in which case, the emperors concerned are Carus and his sons in 282–84, as Zimmerman concludes.[9] Mitchell therefore suggests that these inscriptions should be associated with the unrest in the area that culminated in the siege of Cremna in 278,[10] a conclusion that Zimmerman had reached independently.

---

6. M. Christol, "Un duc dans une inscription de Termessos (Pisidie)," *Chiron* 8 (1978): 529–40.

7. *PLRE* I, Marcianus 22; S. Mitchell, "The Siege of Cremna," in *The Eastern Frontier of the Roman Empire,* ed. D. H. French and C. S. Lightfoot (Oxford, 1989), 311–28; S. Mitchell, *Cremna in Pisidia: An Ancient City in Peace and in War* (London, 1995), 177–218.

8. See J. Reynolds et al., "Roman Inscriptions, 1976–80," *JRS* 71 (1981): 121–52, 128.

9. "Probus, Carus und die Räuber," 271–72.

10. On the siege, see Mitchell, "The Siege of Cremna."

The People

Roman Officials

Aurelius Ursio, perfectissimus dux (I.A.i.1). The name is attested of a
Frankish noble in the sixth century;[11] but it seems most economical to identify this man with a benefactor of Arycanda honored in a recently published
inscription (S. Sahin, *I. Arykanda* [Bonn, 1994], 26):

> τὸν κράτιστον Λ[. . .
> Αὐρ. Οὐρσίωνα [. . .
> πραιτωριανῶν [. . .
> ἡ πόλις τὸν ἑαυτ[ῆς . . .
>   καὶ εὐεργέ[την

The editor suggests reading λ[ογιστής in the first line. The word appeared
to start with Α or Λ. The editor then suggested ἀπὸ πραετοριανῶν in lines
2–3; but Nicholas Milner has now very kindly shown us a newly discovered
inscription from Balboura, which confirms Ursio's titles as *dux* and *tri-
bunus praetorianon.*[12] We might compare Marcianus, attested as a *perfectissimus protector* at Philippopolis under Gallienus, who was τριβοῦνος
πραετωριανῶν καὶ δοῦξ καὶ στρατελάτης.[13] Praetorians are attested in
this area at about this time by honors offered at Termessos to an otherwise
unknown praetorian prefect, Ulpius Silvinus.[14]

> τὸν ἐξοχώτατον
>   ἔπαρχον
> τοῦ ἱεροῦ πραιτωρίου
> [. . . ca. 14–16 . . .]
> 5 [. . . ca. 14–16 . . .]
>   [. . ca. 5–6 . .]
> Οὔλπιον Σιλουῖνον
> ἡ βουλὴ καὶ ὁ δῆμος,
> τὸν σωτῆρα καὶ εὐερ-
> 10 γέτην τῆς πόλεως.

---

11. *PLRE* III, Ursio.
12. N. Milner, "Further Inscriptions from Balboura and the Survey Area no. 9," in *Balboura—A Highland City and Its Territory,* ed. J. Coulton (forthcoming).
13. *PLRE* I, Marcianus 2, from *AE* 1965.114; C. Rouché, "Rome, Asia, and Aphrodisias," *JRS* 71 (1981): 103–20, 116 n. 91.
14. *TAM* III.1.126, pointed out by Stephen Mitchell; the inscription was erected under a single emperor, whose name was erased.

The term *kratistos* is used of both senators and equites at this date.

[–]*lius Aquilinus, perfectissimus hegoumenos* (I.C.ii.17–18). This man writes a letter to the chief villagers. It is difficult to interpret his title as meaning anything other than "governor." An Aquilinus is honored in a verse inscription at Olympus (Lycia).[15]

τὸν στρατιὰς κοσμοῦντα θεηγενέος βασιλῆος,
τὸν πάσης ἀρετῆς ἄξιον ἐκ προγόνων,
ἡ πατρὶς Οὔλυμπος στῆσεν βουλαῖς Ἀκυλεῖνον
κοιναῖς σκεψα⟨μέ⟩νη, βαιὰ χαριζομένη.[16]

While the man honored at Olympus was a local citizen, he had distinguished himself in imperial service, under a single emperor. The editors of *Prosopography of the Later Roman Empire* assumed that his service was elsewhere in the empire; the new evidence suggests that we are already dealing with the phenomenon, common in the later empire, of local citizens serving as governors in their local area. This was routinely forbidden by imperial legislation and could be seen as further evidence of unusual circumstances.

Hermocrates (I.A.ii.3). Apparently the recipient of the series of acclamations asking for Hermaios to remain in office, Hermocrates seems most likely to be a governor, since the acclamations are requesting that Hermaios remain in office κατὰ τὴν κέλευσιν τοῦ ἡγουμέν[ο]υ, "according to the order of the governor."

Valerius Euethios, eparchos (II). This man writes to Kiliortes. The term *eparchos/praefectus* is very vague; a man with the simple title of *eparchos* died fighting brigands ἐν συνπλοκῇ λῃστῶν.[17] It is extremely tempting to identify this man with the Valerius Euethios attested as rationalis/ καθολικός in five papyri and an inscription at Luxor, datable between 302 and 304.[18] If the dating already suggested for these texts is correct, this inscription comes from an earlier period in his career.

Locals

Askoureus (I.A.i.3; I.A.ii.4, 26, 27; III.7). Zimmerman very reasonably conjectured that this might be an ethnic, the name of the village from which

---

15. *PLRE* I, Aquilinus 4.
16. *TAM* II.1173, reconsidered by L. Robert, *Hellenica* IV (Paris, 1948), 36.
17. L. Robert, *Etudes Anatoliennes* (Paris, 1937), 97, from the Bursa Museum.
18. *PLRE* I, Euethius. See Zimmerman, "Probus, Carus und die Räuber," 269–71, for a full discussion.

Hermaios came; but it seems clear from the full text that it is the name of the father of Hermaios.

(M. Aur.) Hermaios (I.A, C, and D; III) This man receives the letter from Ursio (I.A.i.3–4), instructing him to mobilize (?) a group of young men and perhaps lead them to Cremna. That letter gives him no title. He is honored by a city (nameless) with acclamations (I.A.ii) as a brigand chaser. He receives a letter from Aquilinus, addressed to him "and the rest of the *protokometai*" (I.C.ii.19); he appears to be mentioned in I.D.i.3, 16. He appears as the father of the honorand, Kiliortes, in inscription III.

M. Aurelius Kiliortes (II, III). This son of M. Aurelius Hermaios (III) receives a letter from Valerius Euethios, addressed to him as *prooikos* of the *kome* (II). He is honored by the council and people of a city (presumably Termessos) as the high priest of a single Augustus and his Caesars — presumably Carus. He is *axiologotatos* and *endoxotatos* and is described as "protector of the peace," προστάτης εἰρήνης — a relatively rare term, characteristic of the third century, as Zimmerman observes.[19] The similar name *Killortes* is attested at Arycanda of one or more very prominent citizens,[20] at Rhodiapolis in the Opramoas inscription,[21] and at Idebessos.[22]

Mar. Aur. [–]ros (I.C.ii.8). This man can perhaps be identified with Heliodoros (?) (I.C.13).

Heliodoros (?) (I.C.13). This man is possibly the son of Hermaios.

Places

Termessos (I,II). Mentioned twice, as a destination (I.B.i.8, I.D.ii.8) and as the area in which Ovacık is found (II), it is also presumably the πόλις (city) mentioned at I.A.ii, passim and at I.D.i.1, whose officials are the ones there mentioned, and whose council and people were responsible for inscription III.

Cremna (I.A.i.13). Hermaios is to conduct there something/someone, almost certainly the νεανίσκους ἐπιλέκτους, "selected young men," whom he has been instructed to deal with in some way.

Kome (I.C.ii, II). A *kome* is mentioned in I.C.ii. Inscription II is addressed to Kiliortes as *prooikos,* "leading inhabitant," of a *kome.* The name of the community appears in II.2 and apparently in I.C.ii.3 and 22; but, frustratingly, it appears impossible to read more than AΛΛΛEWN in any of these cases. The most reasonable conjecture, therefore, remains Harrison's

19. "Probus, Carus und die Räuber," 273. See also Mitchell, *Cremna in Pisidia,* 34.
20. *I. Arykanda* 44–45, 46 and 48, 79, 111, 120.
21. *TAM* II.905.
22. *TAM* II.838.

'Αδαλεων.[23] The document goes on to refer to brigands who have been cleared away from the area around the *apoikia,* "settlement"; this is apparently another term for the same settlement, but it is an extremely unusual one.[24] Martin Zimmerman reports that the settlement at Ovacık appears to be made up of buildings mostly constructed at about the same time; this and other sites in the region give the impression of being new settlements. It may be that this period saw various kinds of evolution in rural settlements, perhaps experimenting with new institutional structures; this could also provide a context for the petition of Orcistus to Emperor Constantine requesting civic status,[25] as well as providing a backdrop for the emergence of the monastic settlements of the following period.

Komai, "villages" (I.B.i.6).

Offices

Archiereus (III). This is the high priest of the imperial cult, presumably the civic cult at Termessos.

Bouleutes, "councillor" (I.C.ii.9?). This is presumably a member of the city council of Termessos.

Agoranomos (I.D.i.4). This is a standard magistracy in most Greek cities; there is too little context to interpret its function here.

Hypophylax (I.C.ii.15). The ὑποφύλαξ is a title in the Lycian *koinon;* its bearer served under the *archiphylax,* and both officials seem to have been concerned, above all, with ensuring the peaceful operation of the tax-collection system.[26] Zimmerman has studied the office and pointed out that it could be held by relatively modest members of the elite.[27] This is the only identifiable reference to an official of the *koinon.*

Lestodioktes, "brigand chaser" (I.A.ii.10–11, 28). Λῃστοδιώκτης is found in the glossaries, under *latrunculator;* Malalas uses the term of Rheges, a military officer stationed at Caesarea who helped the *dux* of Palestine deal with a Samaritan uprising in or about 484.[28]

23. Pleket and Zimmerman conjectured, very reasonably, that the villagers were the Askoureis, but the argument for *Askoureus* as an ethnic is not supported by the full text. Reger has recently read *Lemeon.*

24. Zimmerman and Schuler have confirmed to us that the term is not otherwise attested in the inscriptions of Asia Minor.

25. The petition is most recently published in A. Chastagnol, "L'inscription constantinienne d'Orcistus," *MEFRA* 93 (1981): 381–416.

26. M. Wörrle, *Stadt und Fest im kaiserzeitliche Kleinasien,* Vestigia 39 (Munich, 1988), 149–50.

27. M. Zimmerman, "Zwischen Polis und Koinon: Zum *Hypophylax* im Lykischen Bund," *Epigraphica Anatolica* 21 (1993): 107–20.

28. John Malalas *Chronicle* 382 and *Chronicon Paschale* 327, with *PLRE* II, Rheges.

Eirenarch, "peacekeeper" (I.A.ii.1; ?I.C.ii.6–7, 16). This is a standard magistracy in Greek cities; see "Municipal Government" later in this appendix.

Neaniskoi, "young men" (I.A.i.7, I.D.ii.14). See "Municipal Government" later in this appendix.

Protokometes, "leading villager" (I.C.ii.21). The earliest example of this term is apparently in a late second-century inscription from Lydia (*TAM* V.822, dated to 198/9); it is found in texts and papyri of the fifth and sixth centuries (so, e.g., at Aphrodito in A.D. 542).[29] By the sixth century it certainly seems to indicate someone with responsibilities for the collection of taxes from the community; it is impossible to say whether this was the case earlier, but it is characteristic of the late Roman period that primacy in a community and fiscal responsibilities should be combined.[30]

Prooikos komes (II). The term *prooikos* has a rather general sense of "person in charge"; its primary use was for administrators of large estates, and it is interesting to see its transfer to, apparently, the preeminent personage of a village. Again, the usage implies the close links between local prominence and responsibilities toward a higher authority.[31]

Historical Setting

The link between these inscriptions is M. Aurelius Hermaios. The purpose of inscription I seems to be to record documents that honor Hermaios. The purpose of inscriptions II and III—which may or may not be later—is to honor Hermaios's son, Kiliortes. He is described (in inscription II) as *prooikos* of his village; but in inscription III he is honored by a city, as a priest of the imperial cult. The city concerned must be Termessos. While the name of the village cannot be made out, it is also apparently referred to as an *apoikia* of the city; its administration is the responsibility of the city of Termessos, as is stressed in the acclamations in inscription I.

The Imperial Government

While the local hierarchy is relatively clear, that at the level of Roman government is less so, since an excessive number of Roman officials seem to be involved. It is simplest to conclude not only that inscriptions II and III are not necessarily contemporary with inscription I but also that the documents in inscription I are not necessarily contemporary with one another.

29. *PCair, Mas* 3, document 67286.
30. On this term, see Schuler, *Ländliche Siedlungen,* 235.
31. See Zimmerman, "Probus, Carus und die Räuber," 277; Schuler, *Ländliche Siedlungen,* 235–36.

It is difficult not to see Aquilinus as a governor. We know that Terentianus Marcianus, *perfectissimus dux,* was in office in 278, when he put up a dedication to Probus at Cremna.[32] Marcianus was also honored at Sagalassos (his hometown), Termessos, and Trebenna, all in Lycia. He appears to be the *hegemon* who led the Roman attack on Cremna when it was being held by rebels — normally described by the authorities as brigands *(lestai)* — under their chief Lydius. He may, therefore, have been the first such appointment, brought in to deal with a particular military problem; but the insurrection at Cremna was only part of a larger peacekeeping problem, as is reflected in these inscriptions.

It may be, therefore, that we should try to fit Ursio, Aquilinus, and Marcianus into a sequence of governors — presumably of Lycia-Pamphylia; perhaps we should add Hermocrates, while Euethios appears to be holding a special military command. But it may be inappropriate to try to impose such order on the shape of the Roman administration at such a difficult period. There are other evidences of unusual commands in Lycia at precisely this period. The bearer of one such command, L. Aurelius Marcianus, was honored at Termessos.[33]

> τὸν διασημότατον δουκ(α)
> Λ. Αὐρ. Μαρκιανὸν
> ἡ βουλὴ καὶ ὁ δῆμος
> τὸν πάτρωνα καὶ εὐεργέτην τῆς
> 5 πόλεως
> καὶ εἰρήνης προστά-
> την

The epithet "protector of the peace" [προστάτης εἰρήνης] is used of Kiliortes in our inscription III. Some years earlier, in the reign of Valerian, Oenoanda honored a certain M. Valerius Statilius Castus, "commander of the vexillations" and "concerned with peace."[34]

> Οὐαλέριον Στατείλιον Κάστον, τὸν κράτιστον σύμμαχον τῶν Σεβα-
> στῶν πραιπόσιτον βιξιλατιώνων, Τερμησσέων τῶν πρὸς Οἰνοάνδοις ἡ
> βουλὴ καὶ ὁ δῆμος καὶ ἡ γερουσία τὸν εὐεργέτην, προνοησάμενον τῆς
> εἰρήνης κατὰ θάλασσαν καὶ κατὰ γῆν, ἐπιδημήσαντα τῇ λαμπρᾷ ἡμῶν
> πόλει μετὰ πάσης εὐκοσμίας.

32. *PLRE* I, Marcianus 22; Mitchell, "The Siege of Cremna" and *Cremna in Pisidia* 208–10.
33. *TAM* III.I.88, reedited by M. Christol in "Un duc."
34. *BCH* (1886): 227, republished as *IGRom* III.481, *ILS* 8870.

At Termessos Maior there are also two inscriptions honoring *kratistoi praepositi,* whose functions are not indicated.

βουλῆς καὶ δή-
μου δόγματι
τὸν κράτιστον
πραιπόσιτον
5   Ἰουστεῖνον
ἡ λαμπρὰ Τερ-
[μησσέων τῶν]
μειζόνων πό-
λις, τὸν ἴδιον αὐ-
10 τῆς ἐν πᾶσιν
εὐεργέτην.

(*TAM* III.80)

βουλῆς καὶ δή-
μου δόγματι τὸν
κράτιστον πραι-
πόσιτον Κωνσταν-
5   τεῖνον ἡ λαμπρὰ
Τερμησσέων τῶν
μειζόνων πόλις,
τὸν ἴδιον αὐτῆς
βουλευτὴν καὶ ἐν
10 πᾶσιν εὐεργέτην.

(*TAM* III.82)

These men are likely to have been in office in the later third century; the Latin title might indicate a military command, but it is in the early fourth century that we first hear of the *praepositi pagorum,* officials responsible for the areas of a city's territory, who seem already to have been well established by 311.[35] The second man mentioned here, Constantinus, is described as a councillor — which presumably means that he was a local citizen; he was very probably responsible for a dedication to the tetrarchs found north of the city.[36]

What seems clear is that a wide range of government representatives, with different titles, were operating in this area in the late third century. It is

35. A. H. M. Jones, *The Later Roman Empire* (Oxford, 1964), 725–26.
36. *TAM* III.943.

also clear that some of those holding offices for the imperial government were in fact local citizens — so Aquilinus and Constantinus. Someone with the title of *dux* or *hegemon* at this period may simply be a governor carrying out normal responsibilities or may be a special officer carrying out specific military functions. Although this region of Asia Minor had had an endemic problem with brigandage, it was only the instability of the mid– to late third century, when the wider security problems of the Roman empire gave new momentum to internal disturbances, that transformed "brigands" into "rebels."[37] These developments focused attention on the function of Roman officials in the provinces. In such a crisis as that in Lycia, the government responded by creating special commands and by replacing governors of senatorial rank with experienced army officers or reliable local notables; it is likely to be these real pressures, rather than some sophisticated policy of excluding senators from office (the so-called Edict of Gallienus), that drove this development in the late third century. More importantly, such circumstances will have drawn attention to the unwieldy size of many of the provinces and encouraged their division into smaller units in a series of reforms that culminated in the reforms of Diocletian.[38]

The Municipal Government

Policing the difficult terrain was a major concern in Lycia; the *koinon* (provincial assembly) of the area appointed policing officials, the *archiphylax* and the *hypophylax,* although their principal responsibility seems to have been ensuring the proper collection of taxes.[39] This did not, however, obviate the need for security enforcement at the city level and in the remote villages. The settlement at Ovacık was evidently within the territory of Termessos. The difficult terrain of the area clearly forced a relatively high level of responsibility for their own safety on the villagers; but the appointment of leaders to organize local defense had to be at least approved by the city. We know that Termessos appointed an *eirenarch* for at least one area of its *territorium,* known as τῶν ἄνω κωμῶν καὶ Δρύμου (*TAM* III.104). Heberdey argued that "the upper villages and the *drymos*" were two of the administrative areas into which the *territorium* was divided;[40] a recently

---

37. See the excellent overview by Mitchell in *Cremna in Pisidia* 211–17.

38. See C. Roueché, "The Functions of the Governor in Late Antiquity: Some Observations," *Antiquité Tardive* 6 (1998): 31–36, for other factors in this process; that article is focused on the civil side of those changes and failed to emphasize sufficiently the security considerations, for which see Roueché, "Rome, Asia, and Aphrodisias."

39. See above, discussion under "offices" and n. 26.

40. R. Heberdey, *Termessische Studien* (Vienna, 1929), 5–15, and "Termessos" in *RE* V.a (1934): 733–37.

published inscription balances this with a reference to a village as being in the lower area, ἐν Νέα Κώμῃ τῇ κάτω.[41]

Hermaios and Kiliortes are not described specifically as *eirenarchs* but seem to be local village leaders who performed very similar functions — Hermaios as a *lestodioktes*, "brigand chaser" (I.A.ii), and Kiliortes as someone who had defeated and captured brigands (II). The language of inscription II is similar to that of a letter of Commodus praising the people of Bubon for the capture and defeat of brigands in their area.

καὶ ὑμᾶς τῆς προθυμίας καὶ τῆς ἀνδρείας ἐπῄνεσα καὶ τὴν κοινὴν βουλὴν τοῦ Λυκίων ἔθνους ἀπεδεξά μην, ὑμᾶς μὲν σὺν τοσαύτῃ τῇ προ- θυμίᾳ ὁρμήσαντας ἐπὶ τὴν τῶν λῃστῶν σύνλημψιν καὶ περιγενομένους γε αὐτῶν καὶ τοὺς μὲν ἀποκτείναντας, τοὺς δὲ καὶ ζωγρήσαντας.[42]

The appointment of *eirenarchs* had to be approved by the governor.[43] This requirement for approval at a higher level was probably intended to guard against abuses. When the people of Hierapolis appointed *paraphylakes*, "guards," for their villages, they were adjured not to obtain more than their designated supplies, and it was stipulated that the *komarchai* must not be forced to "crown" them (i.e., give them money).[44] Those *paraphy- lakes* were posted in the villages for a particular period; their residence there was described as *epidemia*, the term used of the presence of the *lestodioktes* in I.A.ii. Similarly, the proconsul wrote to Aezani how he had thought it suitable ποιήσασθαι τὴν παρ' ὑμῖν ἐπιδημίαν,[45] while a third-century proconsul wrote to the Aphrodisians that he would visit their city as long as there was no imperial ruling that prevented it — κωλύει τὸν ἀνθύπατον ἐπιδημεῖν τῇ πόλει.[46]

Hermaios, therefore, seems to have held an office — that of *lestodioktes* — that was similar to that of the *eirenarch* and subject to the same requirement of approval by the governor, since this is apparently what is being requested in I.A.ii.31: κατὰ τὴν κέλευσιν τοῦ ἡγουμέν[ο]υ ἐπιδημείτω. Despite the

41. B. Iplikçioğlu, G. Çelgin, and V. Çelgin, "Termessos ve Egimenlik Alam Epigrafik," *XV. Araştırma Sonuçları Toplantısı 1997* (1998), 371–81, 374 (pointed out to us by Martin Zimmerman).

42. F. Schindler, *Inschriften von Bubon* (Vienna, 1972), 2.

43. Aristides *Or.* 50.72 and *Cod. Just.* X.77.

44. J. G. C. Anderson, "A Summer in Phrygia: Part 1," *JHS* 17 (1897): 396–425, 403, republished as *OGI* 527.

45. *LBW* 841, republished as *IGRom* IV.572, reconsidered by L. Robert in *Études Anatoliennes*, 301–5.

46. J. Reynolds, *Aphrodisias and Rome* (London, 1981), document 48, lines 21–22.

references to the city, the request is probably that Hermaios should remain in residence at Ovacık. The acclamations are then intended to stress that this is to the advantage of the city as a whole, even if in practice it may involve strengthening and endorsing the power of a local magnate in his own area. It was presumably in that capacity—whether before or after the occasion of the acclamations, we cannot be sure—that he was responsible for gathering a group of "young men," *neaniskoi,* apparently to take them to Cremna, most probably to help the Roman troops besieging that city in 278 (I.A.i). The "young men"—young adults who had finished their training as ephebes—were a recognized group within the city, and they were regularly used in this way. At Apollonia Salbake, a group of "young men" under a *paraphylax* policed the mountains around the city.[47] Despite the dramatic circumstances, therefore, the traditional institutions of the city appear to be functioning in these texts. There is, however, one apparent innovation: the recording of the acclamations in honor of Hermaios.

Acclamations

The set of acclamations here, although it is probably not complete, is one of the longer surviving inscribed series.[48] It has not been edited for inscribing; instead, in its constant repetitions, it resembles the series found in manuscript records—for example, in records of the church councils. This is by far the best preserved section of the inscription.

ὁ ὑπὲρ τῆς πόλεως ἐπιδημείτω.
ὁ ὑπὲρ τῆς εἰρηνης ἐπιδημείτω.
το[ῦ]το cυμφέρει τῇ πόλε[ι].
ψήφιcμα τῷ λῃcτοδ[ει]ώκτῃ.
ὁ εὐγένηc λῃ[c]τοδειώκτηc τὴν π[ό]λιν φρουρείτω.
ὁ λῃcταc φονεύcαc τὴν πόλιν φρουρείτω.
ὁ ἐκδεικήcαc τὴν πόλιν τὴν πόλιν φρουρείτω.

47. J. Robert and L. Robert, *La Carie,* vol. 2, *Le plateau de Tabai* (Paris, 1954), 281–38; C. Roueché, *Performers and Partisans at Aphrodisias* (London, 1993), 123–24, 152.

48. Cf. the acclamations for Albinus at Aphrodisias: see C. Roueché, "Acclamations in the Later Roman Empire: New Evidence from Aphrodisias," *JRS* 74 (1984): 181–99, with a more general discussion; the texts are republished in C. Roueché, *Aphrodisias in Late Antiquity* (London, 1989), nos. 83–84. See also the acclamations of the city of Perge discussed in C. Roueché, *"Floreat Perge," Images of Authority,* ed. M. M. Mackenzie and C. Roueché, Cambridge Philological Society Supplementary Volume 16 (Cambridge, 1989), 206–28, and also discussed by P. Weiss, "Auxe Perge. Beobachtungen zu einem bemerkens werten städtischen Dokument des späten dritten Jahrhunderts," *Chiron* 21 (1991), 353–91.

ὁ πολάκι[ς] ἐκδειϰήςας τὴν π[ό]λιν ἐπιδημείτω.
ὁ ἀ[ν]νώνας ΕΝΝΕϹΑ[. .] πέμψας ἐπιδημεί[τω].
ὁ ὑπὲϱ τῆς [ε]ἰϱή[ν]η[ς] ἐπιδημείτω.
Ἑ[ϱμαι]ος ἐπιδημείτ[ω. ? ὁ υἱ]ὸς Ἀσϰουϱέως ἐ[πιδη]μείτω.
Ἑϱμαιος Ἀ[σ]ϰ[ου]ϱέως ληςτοδει[ώϰ]της ἕως ζῶμεν.
ἐπι[δη]μείτω ἵνα δυνάμεθα [ζῆ]σαι.
ϰατὰ τὴν ϰέλευσιν τοῦ ἡγουμέν[ο]υ ἐπιδημείτω.
ὁ π[ο]λάϰις σώςας τὴν πόλιν ἐπιδη[με]ίτω.
ὁ τϱοφὰς τῇ πόλει πέ[μ]ψας ἐπιδημείτω

[Let him who (acts) on behalf of the city reside! Let him who (acts) on behalf of peace reside! This is of benefit to the city. A decree for the brigand chaser! Let the well-born brigand chaser guard the city! Let him who has killed brigands guard the city! Let him who has often acted as *ekdikos* for the city guard the city! Let him who has acted as *ekdikos* for the city reside! Let him who has . . . sent *annona* reside! Let him who (acts) on behalf of peace reside! Let Hermaios reside; let the son of Askoureus reside! Hermaios, son of Askoureus, as brigand chaser as long as we live! Let him reside so that we can live! Let him reside according to the order of the governor! Let him who has often saved the city reside! Let him who has sent supplies to the city reside!]

There are several typical structures here. For example, the phrasing "he who does so and so, let him . . ." is widely paralleled.

Σεβῆϱος ἄϱτι ἀναθεματισθῆι
ὁ ἐπίβουλος τῆς τϱιάδος ἄϱτι ἀναθεματισθῆι
ὁ ϰατὰ τῶν πατέϱων ἄϱτι ἀναθεματισθῆι
ὁ ἀναθεματίσας τὴν σύνοδον Χαλκηδόνος ἄϱτι ἀναθεματισθῆι.[49]

This repetition of the same phrase in a series of acclamations is also found in our text and must of course have facilitated their use. Another method to make the acclamations flow more easily is to change one half of a sentence and then the other: A + B, A + C, A + D, then D + E, D + F. There is also the occasional recurrence of an earlier line, almost like a refrain. Another characteristic construction is the dative of direction or purpose.

49. Acclamations from Constantinople in 518, reported to the Council of Constantinople in 536; *ACO* III, 73.

Λέοντα τὸν ἐπίσκοπον ῾Ρώμης τοῖς διπτύχοις.

. . . .

τὰ δίπτυχα τῶι ἄμβωνι.[50]

These acclamations therefore follow standard rules; but an even more interesting aspect is their use. They were clearly recorded to be sent to higher
officials, in support of a request for the extension of Hermaios' command.
This foreshadows the ruling by Constantine in 331 that acclamations of provincial assemblies praising or blaming a governor should be conveyed directly
to the emperor.[51] Yet again, the legislation seems to have come in the wake of
the practice. It may be, also, that we are seeing evidence of how the direct use
of acclamations is associated with the development in the late antique period
of new power structures that increasingly bypass civic institutions; it is interesting that another recently discovered set of acclamations, very probably
from about the same period, was recorded on the occasion of the granting of
privileges to a rural community in the territory of Magnesia.[52]

It remains to try to determine the precise function of these acclamations.
The frequent mentions of the *polis* suggest that these were recorded at a
public assembly at Termessos; their presence on the inscription of Ovacık
seems to be as part of a dossier of documents in praise of Hermaios and
does not require him to have been acclaimed there. The presence of the
inscriptions honoring Kiliortes strongly suggests that this was the center of
the family's estates and their power; they are "chief men of the village," but
they also play a part of the life of the city.

Hermaios has been in office for some time; he has "killed brigands" and
has also in some way been responsible for bringing food supplies to the
city — perhaps ensuring their delivery from the countryside to the city when
brigandage was making this difficult. The situation could resemble that in
the mid–sixth century, when the plague was preventing country people from
bringing food to the city of Myra; the citizens saw it as the responsibility of
Nicholas, abbot of the monastery of Sion, to resolve the situation.[53] But
Hermaios is also described as having acted as ἔκδικος. This term is hard to
assess. In the imperial period, it is used of people who have represented a
city as lawyers, and it designates one among many services for which a bene-

---

50. *ACO* III, 74.

51. *Cod. Theod.* I.16.6, repeated as *Cod. Just.* I.40.3; see Roueché, "Acclamations," 186.

52. See the inscription of the Pylitae, published by H. Malay "Letter of the Proconsul Taurus and the
People of Pylitai near Tralles," *Epigraphica Anatolica* 11 (1988): 53–58, with the considerations of
J. Nollé, "Epigraphische und numismatische Notizien 9: zu der neuen Stele aus dem Museum von
Aydin," *Epigraphica Anatolica* 15 (1990): 121–26, and the republication, *SEG* 38 (1988): 1172.

53. *Vita Nicholae Sionitae* 52–57.

factor may be praised. In the fourth century, the term appears describing a new official, called in Latin the *defensor,* who is appointed by the imperial government to judge local cases, offering a fair hearing to people low in the social scale.[54] It may be that the *ekdikos* of the imperial period could sometimes have a similar function; a man is honored in Lydia by the people of two villages whose affairs he had "judged and reestablished": τειμηθέντα τῇ τοῦ ἀνδριάντος ἀναστάσει ὑπὸ Ἀρηνῶν καὶ Ναγδημῶν ἐπὶ τῷ ἐ⟨κ⟩δι-κῆσαι καὶ ἀποκαταστῆσαι τὰ τῶν κωμῶν (*TAM* V.974.7).

It is uncertain whether Hermaios had represented the rights of the city or adjudicated in local disputes, but the latter makes good sense in the circumstances, particularly if these were disputes in the villages where he was operating. We cannot determine whether he performed this function as a representative of the "city," in the old sense of the term, or as an imperial representative, in the late antique sense. Yet again, we are dealing with terminology in transition. This is a useful reminder of the crucible of tensions from which the fourth-century reforms emerged. Local country landowners and their retinues were used by the imperial government to help to maintain peace; local officials were not only appointed subject to imperial approval (as before) but even given direct authority by the imperial government. This may well be the case with Hermaios, both as an *ekdikos* (although we cannot know) and as a "brigand chaser." If the term *lestodioktes* as used by Malalas to describe a situation in the late fifth century has the same force that it had at the end of the third, then Hermaios is not called an *eirenarch* because he is not a civic official but a local citizen appointed by the imperial government to keep the peace in difficult times; he receives instructions directly from Ursio, just as his son receives a letter directly from the *praefectus* Euethios. In both cases the receipt of those letters is enough of a distinction to warrant its inscription.

There is undoubtedly much more to be extracted from these fascinating texts; both our readings and our interpretation leave much room for improvement. One thing that makes them difficult to interpret is that they exemplify a period of evolution, as the settled fabric of the Roman imperial period was transformed into the very different world of late antiquity, which Martin Harrison illuminated with scholarly care.

---

54. The first example is in Egypt in 331; see Jones, *The Later Roman Empire,* 726–27 and n. 31. R. S. Bagnall (*Egypt in Late Antiquity* [Princeton, 1993], 165) emphasizes the continuing uncertainties over the exact role of the *ekdikos;* see, most recently, *POxy* 3771 and commentary there.

Glossary

abacus	Narrow rectangular block, usually square, that forms the topmost element of a capital.
acanthus	Plant with spiky leaves, often used in architectural ornament; where ornament is labeled "windblown acanthus," a strong breeze seems to be blowing the leaves of the plant.
acropolis	Hilltop, usually fortified with walls.
agora	Public square or market place.
ambo	Pulpit, often elliptical in form.
ambo parapet	Low wall around ambo.
apse	Semicircular annex to a building or recess in a wall.
architrave	Lintel in stone or timber carried from the top of one column or pier to another.
ashlar	Regular masonry of squared stones laid in horizontal courses with vertical joints.
atrium	Courtyard constituting the main approach to a church.
baptistery	Usually a separate room entered from one of the aisles of an early Christian church, for baptism of adults by immersion.
barrel vault	Vault in the form of a half-cylinder, as in a continuous arch.
basilica	Oblong rectangular building, usually with nave and lateral aisles.
capital	Topmost member of a column or pilaster.
column drum	Cylindrical section of a column.
conch	Semicircular niche surmounted by a half-dome.

console or corbel	Projecting stone (or timber) support.
cornice	Projecting molding along the top of a building, window, etc.
cross-domed basilica	Building whose core forms a cross and has a dome in the center.
cross-in square structure	Structure divided into nine bays — the center bay a large square, the corner bays small squares, the remaining four bays rectangular. The center bay, resting on four columns, is domed; corner bays are either domed or crown vaulted; rectangular bays are usually barrel vaulted.
Dioskouroi	Deities Castor and Pollux.
Doric	Architectural order originally evolved by the Dorian Greeks, featuring column with base, shaft, and capital.
fosse	Ditch or moat.
hüyük	Artificial mound or tell.
insula	Tenement or apartment block in a city with rectangular plan.
Ionic	Architectural order developed by the Greek cities in Asia Minor, featuring column with base, shaft, and capital.
jamb	Side member of a door frame or window frame.
lintel	Horizontal beam across top of door or window.
martyrium	Site that bears witness to the Christian faith; or structure built on a site associated with the memory of a martyr.
narthex	Vestibule of a church, usually the full width of the church's facade.
necropolis	Cemetery.
niello	Method of ornamenting metal by engraving it and filling up the lines with a black composition.
nymphaeum	Fountain enclosure, usually formed by a series of niches placed against or surmounting a wall.

odeum	Roofed building used for meetings of the town council, musical competitions, etc.
opus sectile	Floor or wall covering consisting of marble slabs cut in a variety of shapes, mainly geometric.
ossuary	Tomb or urn where bones were laid.
pediment	Triangular space, such as a gable, set over a colonnade or other architectural feature.
pendentive	In a square bay defined by four arches of equal diameter and height, whose crowns touch the horizontal seating for a dome, the masonry between adjacent arches that rises to support that seating. The form is triangular, with three concave sides and concave curvature in both vertical and horizontal planes.
piazza	Place or square surrounded by buildings.
pier	Masonry support.
pilaster (engaged column)	Rectangular column or pillar attached to a wall so that some portion of the circumference (usually between a quarter and a half) is cut off by the line of the wall.
podium	Low wall or continuous pedestal on which columns or entire monuments are carried.
polygonal	Used of a wall made of stones with many angles, each stone being shaped and laid to fit tightly with the corresponding angles of its neighbors — an expensive but effective device to reduce the effect of earthquakes.
proskenion	Stone structure consisting of a row of free columns or a row of pillars with engaged columns, standing on a low base about two or three yards in front of the stage building of a theater.
puteal	Wellhead or stone curb placed around the mouth of a well (or, by extension, something that looks similar).
rabbet	Step-shaped reduction cut along an edge or face.
revetment	Facing on a wall.

sanctuary	Chancel, or east end of a church.
sarcophagus	Stone coffin.
scaenae frons	Facade of the stage building that constitutes the backdrop of the stage of an ancient theater.
shard	Fragment of pottery.
soffit	Exposed undersurface of an architectural member.
sondage	Trial excavation.
spolia	Reused architectural pieces.
squinch	Corbeling, usually a small arch, placed across the corners of a square bay to form an octagon suitable for an octagonal or domical roof.
statio	Agency of traders, usually at the docks of a port, e.g., at Ephesus.
stele	Upright slab of stone, usually carved.
stoa	Covered hall, its roof supported by one or more rows of columns parallel to the rear wall.
stratigraphy	Study and interpretation of archaeological strata or layers.
synthronon	In a Byzantine church, bench or benches for the clergy, built in a semicircle in the apse.
tabula ansata	Literally, "a panel with handles."
templon	Trabeated colonnade above the chancel of a church, dividing the nave from the sanctuary.
territorium	Countryside surrounding a city, including villages and farms that belong to that city.
tesserae	Small cubes of stone, glass, etc. used in mosaic work.
theme	Originally referring to a body of soldiers, this term was extended to refer to the district where the body was stationed. The theme was governed by a *strategos* (general), who was in charge of both civil and military administration.
trabeated	Composed of horizontal and vertical members, not arched or vaulted.
transept	Transverse unit of a basilical plan, as a rule inserted between nave and apse.

triconchos   Used of a church (or other building) with
                            apses *(conches)* on three sides of a square
                            bay.

tympanum   Vertical back wall closing a pediment.

vault   Roof or ceiling of brick or stone, supported
                            on the principle of the arch; or a roof of simi-
                            lar shape constructed of a mass of concrete.

voussoir   Brick or wedge-shaped stone that forms one
                            of the vaults of an arch.

Bibliography

Anrich, G. *Der heilige Nikolaos in der griechischen Kirche.* Vols. 1–2. Leipzig and Berlin, 1913–17.

Aran, B. "Antalya Cumanun Camisi." *Anadolu Sanatı Araştırmaları* 2 (1970): 60–76.

Bakker, G. "The Buildings at Alahan." In *Alahan: An Early Christian Monastery in S. Turkey,* ed. M. Gough, 75–153. Toronto, 1985.

Ballance, M. H. "Cumanın Cami'i at Antalya: A Byzantine Church." *PBSR* 23, n.s. 10 (1955): 99–114.

Bayburtluoğlu, C. Brief reports on archaeological work at Arykanda. *Archaeology in Asia Minor,* annual reports ed. M. J. Mellink, *AJA* 76–96 (1972–92).

———. "Arykanda." In *Princeton Encyclopedia of Classical Sites,* ed. R. Stillwell, 98. Princeton, 1976.

Bean, G. E. "The site of Podalia." *Anzeiger der phil. hist. Klasse des Österreichischen Akademie der Wissenschaften* 8 (1968): 157–63.

———. "Journeys in Northern Lycia." *Denkschrift Österreichischen Akademie* 104 (1971): 28–32.

———. *Lycian Turkey.* London, 1978.

Bean, G. E., and R. M. Harrison. "Choma in Lycia." *JRS* 57 (1967): 40–44.

Benndorf, O., and G. Niemann. *Reisen im südwestlichen Kleinasien.* Vol. 1, *Reisen in Lykien und Karien.* Vienna, 1884.

Bobčev, S. N. "Die Stadtmauertürme mit spitzem Vorsprung und ihre Bedeutung für die Befestigung der antike Städte." *Bulletin de l'Institut Archéologique Bulgare* 24 (1961): 103–45.

Borchhardt, J. "Limyra, 1973." *AS* 24 (1974): 40–41.

———. "Limyra, 1974." *AS* 25 (1975a): 32–34.

Borchhardt, J., ed. *Myra: Eine Lykische Metropole in antiker und byzantinischer Zeit.* Istanbuler Forschungen 30. Berlin, 1975b.

Canard, M. "Ammuriye." In *Encyclopaedia of Islam,* 1:462. 2d ed. Leiden, 1960.

Darrouzès, J. *Géographie ecclésiastique de l'empire byzantin.* Vol. 1, *Notitiae Episcopatuum Ecclesiae Constantinopolitae.* Paris, 1981.

Davis, E. J. *Anatolica.* London, 1874.

Demargne, P., and H. Metzger. *Guide de Xanthos.* Ankara, 1966.

Demargne, P., et al. *Fouilles de Xanthos.* 9 vols. to date. Paris, 1958–.

De Planhol, X. *De La Plaine Pamphylienne aux lacs Pisidiens: Nomadisme et Vie Paysanne.* Bibliothèque Archéologique de l'Institut Français d'Istanbul 3. Paris, 1958.

Dodge, H., and B. Ward-Perkins, eds. *Marble in Antiquity: Collected Papers of J. B. Ward-Perkins.* Archaeological Monographs of the British School at Rome, no. 6. London, 1992.

Dumbarton Oaks Research Library and Collection. *Handbook of the Byzantine Collection.* Washington, D.C., 1967.

Farrington, A., and J. J. Coulton. "Terracotta Spacer Pins in Lycian Bath Buildings." *AS* 40 (1990): 55–67.

Fellows, C. *Travels and Researches in Asia Minor, More Particularly in the Province of Lycia.* London, 1852.

Ferrari, G. *Il commercio dei sarcofagi attici.* Rome, 1966.

Fıratlı, N. "Un trésor du VIe s. trouvé a Kumluca en Lycie." *Akten des VII Internationalen Kongresses für Christliche Archäologie,* 1965, 523–25.

———. "Excavations at Selçikler (Sebaste) in Phrygia." *Yayla* 2 (1979): 18–21.

Foss, C. "The Persians in Asia Minor and the End of Antiquity." *English Historical Review* 90 (1975): 721–47.

———. *Byzantine and Turkish Sardis.* Harvard, 1976.

———. *Survey of Medieval Castles of Anatolia.* Vol. 1, *Kütahya.* British Institute of Archaeology at Ankara Monograph. London, 1985.

Fraser, P. M., and E. Matthews, eds. *A Lexicon of Greek Personal Names.* Vol. 1, *The Aegean Islands, Cyprus, Cyrenaica.* Oxford, 1987.

Garstang, J., and O. R. Gurney. *The Geography of the Hittite Empire.* London, 1959.

Grassi, G. "Precisazioni sulla Panaghía di Antalya." In *Milion,* ed. C. Barsanti et al., Studi e Ricerche d'Arte Bizantina 1. Rome, 1989.

Greenhalgh, J. "Late Roman Pisidia." Ph.D. diss., University of Newcastle upon Tyne, 1987.

Grossman, P., and H. G. Severin. "Forschungen in Südöstlichen Lykien." *Türk Arkeoloji Dergisi* 25, 2 (1981): 101–10.

Hamilton, W. J. *Researches in Asia Minor.* London, 1842.

Harrison, R. M. "Four Early Christian Monasteries in Central Lycia." *AS* 10 (1960a): 26–28.

———. "New Discoveries in Lycia: Four Early Christian Monasteries." *Illustrated London News,* 20 Aug. 1960b, 305–6.

———. "Early Byzantine Remains in Lycia." *AS* 11 (1961): 6–7.

———. "Churches and Chapels of Central Lycia." *AS* 13 (1963): 117–51.

———. "Lycia, 1963." *AS* 14 (1964): 10.

———. Report on the church at the Xanthos Letöon. Unattributed. See H. Metzger, "Fouilles du Létoon de Xanthos (1962–65)," *RA* n.s., fasc. 1 (1966): 109–11.

———. "A Note on Architectural Sculpture in Central Lycia." *AS* 22 (1972): 187–97.

———. "Lycia in Late Antiquity." *Yayla* 1 (1977): 10–15.

———. "Lycian Survey." In *Archaeology in Asia Minor,* annual reports ed. M. J. Mellink, *AJA* 82 (1978): 335–37.

———. "Aspects of Late Roman and Early Byzantine Lycia." *Türk Tarih Kongresi* (1979a): 525–31.

———. "Nouvelles Découvertes Romaines Tardives et Paléobyzantines en Lycie." *CRAI,* 1979b, 222–39.

———. "Upland Settlements in Early Medieval Lycia." *ACLA* 1980: 109–18.

———. "The Alakilise Valley in Lycia 1977." *Türk Arkeoloji Dergisi,* 1981, 111–15.

———. "Survey in Central Lycia." *Araştırma Sonuçları Toplantısı* (1984): 75–77.

———. "An Ambo Parapet in the Antalya Museum." *Studien zur Spätantiken und Byzantinischen Kunst* 10 (1986a): 73–74.

———. *Excavations at Saraçhane in Istanbul.* Vol. 1, *The Excavations, Structures, Architectural Decoration, Small Finds, Coins, Bones, and Molluscs.* Princeton and Washington, D.C., 1986b.

———. "Amorium, 1987: A Preliminary Survey." *AS* 38 (1988): 175–84.

———. "Amorium, 1988: The First Preliminary Excavation." *AS* 39 (1989a): 167–74.

———. *A Temple for Byzantium.* London, 1989b.

Harrison, R. M., and G. R. J. Lawson. "An Early Byzantine Town at Arif in Lycia." *Yayla* 2 (1979): 13–17.

Harrison, R. M., et al. "Amorium Excavations, 1989: The Second Preliminary Report." *AS* 40 (1990): 205–18.

———. "Amorium Excavations, 1990: The Third Preliminary Report." *AS* 41 (1991): 215–29.

———. "Amorium Excavations, 1991: The Fourth Preliminary Report." *AS* 42 (1992): 207–22.

———. "Excavations at Amorium: 1992 Interim Report." *AS* 43 (1993): 147–62.

Hayes, J. W. *Late Roman Pottery.* London, 1972.

Hill, S. "Dağ Pazarı and Its Monuments: A Preliminary Report." *Yayla* 2 (1979): 8–12.

Jones, A. H. M. *The Cities of the Eastern Roman Provinces.* 2d ed. Oxford, 1971.

Jones, C. W. *Saint Nicholas of Myra, Bari, and Manhattan: Biography of a Legend.* Chicago, 1978.

Lambrechts, P. Annual reports on archaeological work at Pessinus. *AS* 20–23 (1970–73).

Lauffer, S. *Diokletian's Preisedikt.* Berlin, 1971.

Magie, D. *Roman Rule in Asia Minor.* Princeton, 1950.

Mainstone, R. J. *Hagia Sophia.* London, 1988.

Mango, C. "Isaurian Builders." In *Polychronion (Festschrift Franz Dölger zum 75 Geburtstag),* 358–65. Heidelberg, 1966.

———. *Byzantium: The Empire of New Rome.* London, 1980.

Mellink, M. J. "The Early Bronze Age in Southwest Anatolia: A Start in Lycia." *Archaeology* 22 (1969): 290–99.

———. "The Painted Tomb near Elmalı." *AJA* 74 (1970): 251–53.

———. "The Kızılbel Tomb." *AJA* 75 (1971): 246–55.

———, ed. *Archaeology in Asia Minor.* Annual reports. *AJA* 59–97 (1955–93).

Metzger, H. "Les Défenses de l'Acropole." In *Fouilles de Xanthos,* vol. 2, *L'Acropole Lycienne,* ed. H. Metzger, 1–14. Paris, 1963.

———. "Fouilles du Létoon de Xanthos (1962–65)." *RA* n.s., fasc. 1 (1966): 101–12.

———. "Xanthos, 1970." *AS* 21 (1971): 58.

Mitchell, S. et al. Annual reports on archaeological work at Cremna. *AS* 37–39 (1987–89).

———. Annual reports on archaeological work at Sagalassos. *AS* 37– (1987–).

Morganstern, J. *The Byzantine Church at Dereağzı and Its Decoration.* Istanbuler Mitteilungen 29. Tübingen, 1983.

Naumann, R. Annual reports on archaeological work at Aezani. *Arch. Anz.,* 1980, 123–36; 1982, 345–82; 1984, 453–530; 1987, 301–58.

Pertusi, A., ed. *Constantino Porfirogenito de Thematibus.* Rome, 1952.

Peschlow, U. "Die Architektur der Nikolaoskirche in Myra." *Myra: Eine Lykische Metropole in antiker und byzantinischer Zeit,* ed. J. Borchhardt, 303–59. Istanbuler Forschungen 30. Berlin, 1975.

Petersen, E., and F. von Luschan. *Reisen im Südwestlichen Kleinasien.* Vol. 2, *Reisen in Lykien, Milyas, und Kibyratien.* Vienna, 1889.

Radet, G. "Les Villes de la Pisidie." *RA* 22 (1893): 185–218.

Radt, W. "Pergamon." In *Archaeology in Asia Minor,* annual reports ed. M. J. Mellink, *AJA* 84 (1980): 514.

Ramsay, W. M. "Inscriptions inédites de marbres phrygiens." *Mélanges d'Archéologie et d'Histoire* 2 (1882): 290–301.

———. *Historical Geography of Asia Minor.* London, 1890.

Rickman, G. *Roman Granaries and Store Buildings.* Cambridge, 1971.

Robert, L. "Villes et Monnaies de Lycie." *Hellenika* 10 (1955): 188–222.

————. "Lettres Byzantines: Les Kordakia de Nicée, le Combustible de Synnada et les Poissons Sciès sur des lettres d'un métropolite de Phrygie au Xe siècle, philologie et réalités." *Journal des Savants,* 1962, 5–74.

Rott, H. *Kleinasiatische Denkmäler aus Pisidien, Pamphylien, Kappadokien und Lykien.* Leipzig, 1908.

Runciman, S. "The Early Tribulations of a Byzantinist." In Ανασκαφες (Excavations): *A Celebration of the Centenary of the British School at Athens, 1886–1986.* London, 1986.

Russell, J. "Byzantine *Instrumenta Domestica* from Anemurium: The Significance of Context." In *City, Town, and Countryside in the Early Byzantine Era,* ed. R. L. Hohlfelder, 134. New York, 1982.

Ševčenko, I., and N. P. Ševčenko. *The Life of St. Nicholas of Sion: Text and Translation.* Massachusetts, 1984.

Ševčenko, N. P. *The Life of St. Nicholas in Byzantine Art.* Turin, 1983.

Severin, H.-G. "Alacadağ, 1976." *AS* 27 (1977): 23–24.

Sodini, J.-P. Annual reports on the Xanthos basilica. *Türk Arkeoloji Dergisi* 19 (1970): 171; 20 (1973): 119–21; 21 (1974): 133–34. Reprinted in *Archaeology in Asia Minor,* annual reports ed. M. J. Mellink, *AJA* 75–77 (1971–73), 80–82 (1976–78).

Spieser, J.-M. *Thessalonique et ses Monuments du IVe au VIe Siècle: Contribution a l'étude d'une ville paléochrétienne.* Athens, 1984.

Spratt, T. A. B., and E. Forbes. *Travels in Lycia, Milyas, and the Cibyratis.* Vol. 1 London, 1847.

Texier, C. *Description de L'Asie Mineure.* Vol. 3. Paris, 1849.

Treadgold, W. *The Byzantine Revival,* A.D. *780–842.* Stanford, 1988.

Vasiliev, A. A. *Byzance et les Arabes.* Vol. 1. Brussels, 1935.

Waelkens, M. *Dokimeion: Die Werkstatt der repräsantativen Kleinasiatischen Sarkophage, Chronologie und Typologie ihrer Produktion.* Archäologische Forschungen 11. Berlin, 1982.

————. *Die Kleinasiatischen Türsteine.* Mainz, 1986.

Ward-Perkins, J. B. "Nicomedia and the Marble Trade." *PBSR* 48 (1980): 23–69.

Wörrle, M. "Die Horrea Hadriani in Andriake." In *Myra: Eine Lykische Metropole in antiker und byzantinischer Zeit,* ed. J. Borchhardt, 66–71. Istanbuler Forschungen 30. Berlin, 1975.

Wurster, W. W. "Antike Siedlungen in Lykien." *Arch. Anz.,* 1976, 23–49.

Wurster, W. W., and M. Wörrle. "Die Stadt Pinara." *Arch. Anz.,* 1978, 74–101.

Supplementary Bibliography of Works
Published since 1992

Borchhardt, J., and G. Dobesch, eds. *Akten des 11. Internationalen Lykien-Symposions, Wien, 6–12 Mai 1990.* Vols. 1 and 2. Österreichischen Akademie der Wissenschaften. Vienna, 1993. This work includes: J. Morganstern, "The Settlement at Dereağzı: An Introduction to the History of the Site" (2:71–76); C. Bayburtluoğlu, "Arycanda" (2:119–24); R. Jacobek, "Lykien-Bibliographie" (2:245–314).

Boyd, S., and M. M. Mango. *Ecclesiastical Silver Plate in Sixth-Century Byzantium.* Pt. 1, *The Sion Treasure.* Dumbarton Oaks Research Library and Collection. Washington, D.C., 1992.

Canbilen, H., P. Lebouteiller, and J.-P. Sodini. Report on the the Xanthos basilica. *Anatolia Antiqua* 4 (1996): 201–29.

Farrington, A. *Roman Bath Buildings in Lycia.* British Institute of Archaeology at Ankara Monograph. London, 1995.

Foss, C. *Cities, Fortresses, and Villages of Byzantine Asia Minor.* Aldershot, 1996. This collection includes the following articles by Professor Foss: "Lycia in History"; "The Lycian Coast in the Byzantine Age"; "Cities and Villages of Lycia in the Life of St. Nicholas of Holy Zion."

Gates, M.-H., ed. *Archaeology in Turkey.* Annual reports. *AJA* 98– (1994–). Includes notes on work proceeding at Arykanda, Balboura, Demre/Myra, Limyra, Patara, Sagalassos, Xanthos, and the Letöon.

Hill, S. *The Early Byzantine Churches of Cilicia and Isauria.* Birmingham Byzantine and Ottoman Monographs, vol. 1. Aldershot, 1996.

Işık, F. Report on a monument from Patara dedicated to Emperor Claudius by Q. Veranius, military governor of this region. In *Archaeology in Turkey,* annual reports ed. M.-H. Gates, *AJA* 100 (1996): 314. Lists roads connecting Patara to other towns in the area.

Knoblauch, P., and C. Winkel. "Arykanda in Lykien. Eine topographische Aufnahme." *Arch. Anz.* 1993: 229–69.

Lightfoot, C. S. "Amorium." *Minerva* 5, no. 1 (1994): 14–16.

———. "Excavations at Amorium." *Anatolian Archaeology* 1 (1995): 5–7.

———. "Amorium." *Anatolian Archaeology* 2 (1996): 8–9.

———. "Amorium." *Anatolian Archaeology* 3 (1997): 6–7.

Lightfoot, C. S., et al. "Amorium Excavations, 1993: The Sixth Preliminary Report." *AS* 44 (1994): 105–28, pls. 17–24.

———. "Amorium Excavations, 1994: The Seventh Preliminary Report." *AS* 45 (1995): 105–38, pls. 13–20.

————. "Amorium Excavations, 1995: The Eighth Preliminary Report." *AS* 46 (1996): 91–110, pls. 12–14.

Mitchell, S. "Archaeology in Asia Minor 1990–98." *Archaeological Reports for 1998–1999.* Society for the Promotion of Hellenic Studies and the British School at Athens. London, 1999. See especially reports on Myra (p. 168), Alakilise (p. 168), Limyra (p. 169), Arykanda (p. 170), Choma (p. 170), Islâmlar (p. 170), Sagalassus (p. 176), Aezani (p. 180) and Amorium (pp. 181–83).

Mitchell, S., et al. *Cremna in Pisidia: An Ancient City in Peace and in War.* London, 1995.

Morganstern, J., ed. *The Fort at Dereağzı and Other Material Remains in Its Vicinity from Antiquity to the Middle Ages.* Istanbuler Forschungen 40. Tübingen, 1993. See, in that volume, app. 2, "New Sculpture and Furnishings from the Church Complex at Dereağzı," 174–76, for comparison of sculpture with that from Alaca Dağ; see also, in the same volume, D. French, "The Road, Paths, and Water Channel," 87–90.

Ötuken, S. Y. "1995 yılı Demre Aziz Nikolaos Kilisesi Kazısı." *XVIII Kazı Sonuçları Toplantısı* II 1996 (1997), 471–87.

Özgen, İlknur. Reports on excavations at Hacımusalar (the site of Choma). In *Archaeology in Turkey,* annual reports ed. M.-H. Gates, *AJA* 100 (1996): 315; 101 (1997): 282.

Research Group for Byzantine Lycia. *Island of St. Nicholas: Excavation of Gemiler Island on Mediterranean Coast of Turkey.* Japan, 1998.

Tsuji, S. "The Survey of Early Byzantine Sites in Ölü Deniz Area (Lycia, Turkey): The First Preliminary Report." *Memoirs of the Faculty of Letters, Osaka University* 35 (1995).

Waelkens, M., ed. *Sagalassos I: First General Report on the Survey (1986–89) and Excavations (1990–91).* Louvain, 1993.

Index

DATE DUE

GAYLORD		PRINTED IN U.S.A.